THE AUSTRALIAN
Women's Weekly
wok simple

acp
books

CONTENTS

WOK ESSENTIALS

Stir-frying is a quick, easy, healthy style of cooking, but you need to have some basic equipment and follow a few golden rules. Pay a visit to just about any Asian food store and it will have all the equipment you'll need.

WHICH WOK TO BUY

An inexpensive pressed metal wok will work just as well, if not better, than many of the more expensive varieties. Check the handle/s to see and feel what's comfortable for you. A long wooden heatproof handle is sufficient on a small to medium-sized wok, as these can be easily managed. For larger, heavier woks, however, you will need two handles to be able to move the wok over the heat – these are usually made from metal, so they will get very hot. Consider the size of the wok you need. These days, many families don't eat together, so it might be better to buy a smaller wok, just large enough to stir-fry food for one or two people. It's important the wok you choose is compatible with your cooktop, check the manufacturer's manual for this information. You might need a flat-bottomed wok, or one that will sit in a ring over the heat source. Woks are barbecue-friendly; some barbecues have a wok burner attached to them, however, make sure the wok you buy is suitable for your particular barbecue.

WOK ACCESSORIES

A wok chan – a lifter and stirrer – fits the shape of the wok, and while a chan isn't vital to have, it's a comfortable utensil to use to toss and move the food around. It's not essential to have a *lid*, but it's very useful. Buy one that fits the wok tightly, as this will trap the steam and heat. This is especially handy for seafood, like mussels, prawns etc, where high heat is needed to cook the seafood quickly without toughening it. Also, for a quick wilting of Asian greens, the lid does wonders. *A wok ring* holds the wok steady. For electric cooktops, buy a solid-metal design with ventilation holes. For gas, a wire-frame will ensure the flame gets enough air. There are other pieces of equipment you can buy, including super-long chopsticks for turning food over during cooking, strainers, steamers, lifters and so on, but a wok and a chan are enough to start with. (See inside the flaps for more information.)

SEASONING YOUR WOK

Your new wok will need to be seasoned before you use it. If you can, do this on a barbecue outside as seasoning causes a lot of smoke. There are lots of theories about seasoning a wok, but basically you are trying to build a patina of oil over the inside surface, which will cause the wok to blacken; you will find that food will almost never stick to a much-used wok. Wash the wok well with hot soapy water, then rinse and dry it. Dab some peanut oil (it's the best oil to use over high heat) onto a wad of absorbent paper and wipe it over the entire inside surface of the wok – the coating of oil should be light and even. Place the wok over the heat source, turn the heat to low then increase the heat gradually to a moderately high temperature, or until the oil starts to smoke. It works best if you oil and heat the wok a couple of times, leaving it to cool down completely before going through the process again. After cooking, cool the wok, wash it with hot soapy water using a brush to remove any stubborn pieces of food (don't scour the wok), rinse and dry it well. To dry the wok completely, put it over a low heat for a few minutes. If not using the wok for a while, wipe the inside surface lightly with oil, or spray with cooking oil, then cover the surface with plastic wrap to prevent dust settling on the oil. This will stop any rust developing on the surface. Remove the plastic, wash, rinse and dry the wok before using it again.

STIR-FRY EXPRESS

You can get away with stir-frying in a frying pan, it's just not as easy to handle a pan as it is a wok. Also, there is a tendency to "stir" and squash the food, as opposed to keeping the food on the move during the tossing action of stir-frying. It's quite difficult to toss the food and keep it moving in a pan, whereas it's easy to do this in a wok using a chan. The cooking time is minimal, so your family should be ready, chopsticks in hand, to eat. There's nothing quite so grim-looking as a stir-fry that's cooled down. Think about how stir-fries are cooked in a restaurant; they use a large wok over an extremely high heat, in which they cook a relatively small amount of food. Never overload a wok with food, this will only cause the temperature of the wok to drop and the food to turn soggy. Don't forget to have rice, noodles etc, ready too.

KNOW YOUR SAUCE

LIGHT SOY has a thin consistency, is light in colour and saltier than dark soy. It's used when the natural colour of the ingredient is important to the dish. It's also used as a condiment and is good in soups, and with fish, chicken and pork.

DARK SOY has a thick consistency and is less salty than light soy. It has a robust malty flavour and is usually coloured with caramel. It's used in braises, stews and casseroles that contain red or game meat.

JAPANESE SOY is also known as tamari. It is a naturally fermented soy sauce and has a low percentage of wheat compared to most other soy sauces. It has an intense, but clean, flavour, and is used in cooking and for dipping sauces. It's great with sashimi-quality fish and oily fish.

KECAP MANIS is an Indonesian soy sauce sweetened with palm sugar; it's also sometimes flavoured with star anise and garlic. It's used in cooking, mostly with red meat, and as a dipping sauce. It's often used as a substitute for dark soy.

KECAP ASIN originated in Indonesia, and is known as 'salty soy sauce'; it is very similar in taste to the Chinese light soy sauce, although it is slightly thicker and has a stronger flavour. It goes well with white fish.

FISH is made from the juice leftover from salted anchovies or squid. There are many varieties: some are light in flavour and make good dipping sauces, others are strong and are best used in cooking. It's an acquired taste, always salty, and should be used in small quantities to begin with.

HOISIN is made from salted, fermented soya beans, onions and garlic. It's thick, with a slightly sweet spicy flavour. Used as a marinade, and is part of the sweet, sticky flavour of chinese barbecued duck and pork. Hoisin is served with peking duck, a dish that is prized for its thin, crispy skin.

PLUM is sticky with a sweet and sour flavour; it is mostly used in Chinese cooking as a dip for deep-fried foods, or as an ingredient in a marinade.

BLACK BEAN is a strong-flavoured salty sauce made from fermented soya beans. It's used as an ingredient in sauces and marinades for all kinds of seafood and meat dishes. Always use it sparingly to begin with.

OYSTER is an all-purpose seasoning that goes well with all kinds of meat and seafood, and steamed asian vegetables, often as an ingredient in a sauce or marinade. It's made from oysters, soy sauce, salt and spices.

CHILLI there are many varieties available, all based on chillies. It's used in cooking and as a condiment. It goes well with almost all savoury foods. The degree of heat of this sauce varies hugely, so be careful of how much you use.

CHILLI BEAN is a spicy, salty sauce made from fermented broad beans, soya beans, rice, chillies and various spices. It goes well with stir-fried vegetables and fried rice.

SWEET CHILLI is made from chillies with added sugar. It's popular in most western countries and goes well with prawn toast, spring rolls and chicken dishes. It's fast becoming the "new" tomato sauce.

TERIYAKI, traditionally, was a cooking technique in which food was marinaded in a mixture of sweet soy sauce, sake, ginger, sugar and various seasonings, then grilled or fried. The commercially made sauce contains the same ingredients. It goes well with chicken and most other meat.

CHAR SIU is a Chinese barbecue sauce made of hoisin, sherry, soy, sugar, black bean paste and five spice. It was traditionally made to go with roasted pork, but is excellent used as a glaze for ham, or with duck and lamb.

XO is made from chopped dried seafood cooked with chilli, garlic, onion and oil; serve a little as a sauce with any seafood. The name comes from fine XO (extra old) cognac, a liqueur thought to denote high quality or prestige; so XO was used to suggest the same high-quality of the sauce.

STIR-FRIES FOR ONE

on the table in 25 MIN

TURKEY LARB WITH CRANBERRIES

1 tablespoon peanut oil
1 clove garlic, crushed
1 shallot (25g), chopped finely
1 tablespoon dried cranberries, chopped coarsely
200g turkey mince
1 tablespoon light soy sauce
½ teaspoon fish sauce
1 tablespoon kecap manis
½ teaspoon five-spice powder
1 small carrot (70g), grated finely
1 cup (80g) finely shredded wombok
½ lebanese cucumber (65g), seeded, sliced thinly
1 fresh long red chilli, sliced thinly
1 lime wedge

1 Heat oil in wok; stir-fry garlic, shallot and cranberries until shallots are tender. Add mince; stir-fry until mince changes colour.
2 Add sauces, five-spice, carrot and wombok; stir-fry until wombok wilts, season to taste.
3 Serve larb topped with cucumber, chilli and lime.
nutritional count per serving 29.4g total fat (6.9g saturated fat); 2157kJ (516 cal); 17.1g carbohydrate; 42.3g protein; 7.4g fibre

Chicken or pork mince can be used instead of turkey mince.

on the table in # 30 MIN

ASPARAGUS WITH GREEN BEANS, EGG AND TOFU

130g silken firm tofu, cut into 2cm pieces
3 teaspoons white miso paste
2 teaspoons grated palm sugar
¼ cup (60ml) warm water
1 tablespoon peanut oil
1 shallot (25g), sliced thinly
170g asparagus, trimmed, halved lengthways
100g green beans, trimmed, halved lengthways
1 teaspoon peanut oil, extra
1 egg
1 fresh small red thai chilli, sliced thinly
½ green onion, sliced thinly

1 Spread tofu, in single layer, on absorbent-paper lined tray; cover with more paper, stand 10 minutes.
2 Meanwhile, combine miso paste, sugar and the water in small bowl.
3 Heat oil in wok; stir-fry shallot, asparagus and beans until vegetables are tender. Add miso mixture and tofu; stir-fry until hot, season to taste.
4 Meanwhile, heat extra oil in small frying pan; fry egg, one side only, until barely set.
5 Serve stir-fry topped with egg, chilli and onion.
nutritional count per serving 32.7g total fat (6.5g saturated fat); 2065kJ (494 cal); 18.9g carbohydrate; 27.9g protein; 8.5g fibre

on the table in **30 MIN**

Serve with steamed rice.
Beef mixture can be marinated for a few hours
or overnight in the fridge.

BEEF TERIYAKI WITH PAK CHOY

200g beef strips
¼ cup (60ml) teriyaki sauce
1cm piece fresh ginger (5g), grated
1 fresh small red thai chilli, sliced thinly
1 tablespoon peanut oil
1 shallot (25g), chopped finely
½ small red capsicum (75g), chopped finely
1 baby pak choy (150g), chopped coarsely
¼ cup (20g) bean sprouts

1 Combine beef, sauce, ginger and chilli in small bowl.
2 Drain beef; reserve marinade. Heat half the oil in wok; stir-fry beef until browned. Remove from wok
3 Heat remaining oil in wok; stir-fry shallot and capsicum until capsicum is tender. Add pak choy and reserved marinade; stir-fry until sauce boils and pak choy wilts, season to taste. Serve topped with sprouts.

nutritional count per serving 23.1g total fat
(4.9g saturated fat); 2073kJ (496 cal);
7.3g carbohydrate; 61.5g protein; 3.9g fibre

on the table in # 30 MIN

CUMIN SQUID WITH TAMARIND DRESSING

1 cleaned squid hood (150g)
1 clove garlic, crushed
1 tablespoon finely grated lemon rind
½ teaspoon ground cumin
½ teaspoon dried chilli flakes
½ teaspoon sweet paprika
1 tablespoon peanut oil
½ small red onion (50g), sliced thinly
1 small zucchini (90g), halved lengthways,
   sliced thinly
60g baby spinach leaves
TAMARIND DRESSING
1 tablespoon tamarind concentrate
1 teaspoon honey
1 tablespoon warm water

1 Cut squid down centre to open out; score inside in diagonal pattern then cut squid into thick strips. Combine squid, garlic, rind and spices in small bowl.
2 Make tamarind dressing.
3 Heat half the oil in wok; stir-fry squid until browned lightly and tender. Remove from wok.
4 Heat remaining oil in wok; stir-fry onion and zucchini until vegetables are tender. Add spinach; stir-fry until wilted, season to taste. Serve drizzled with tamarind dressing.
tamarind dressing Combine ingredients in small bowl.
nutritional count per serving 20.7g total fat (3.9g saturated fat); 1626kJ (389 cal); 20.1g carbohydrate; 28.7g protein; 4.8g fibre

Cuttlefish or scallops would be an excellent substitute for the squid. Squid mixture can be marinated for a few hours or overnight in the fridge.

on the table in # 30 MIN

SATAY CHICKEN

1 tablespoon peanut oil
250g chicken tenderloins, sliced thickly
½ small brown onion (40g), chopped finely
1 fresh small red thai chilli, sliced thinly
3 teaspoons no-added salt crunchy peanut butter
¼ cup (60ml) coconut milk
1 teaspoon light soy sauce
2 teaspoons honey
1 small carrot (70g), cut into matchsticks
1 tablespoon finely chopped fresh coriander
1 tablespoon coarsely chopped roasted
   unsalted peanuts
½ green onion, sliced thinly

1 Heat oil in wok; stir-fry chicken, brown onion and chilli until chicken is browned.
2 Add peanut butter, coconut milk, sauce, honey and carrot; stir-fry until chicken is cooked and carrot is tender. Remove from heat; stir in coriander, season to taste. Serve sprinkled with nuts and green onion.

nutritional count per serving 49.6g total fat (17.7g saturated fat); 3377kJ (808 cal); 22.4g carbohydrate; 66.4g protein; 6.6g fibre

Serve with steamed jasmine rice.
Use light coconut milk for a lower-fat sauce.
Use crushed or granulated peanuts if you prefer.

on the table in # 30 MIN

CHAR SIU PORK WITH SNAKE BEANS

200g pork strips
2 tablespoons char siu sauce
2 teaspoons light soy sauce
1 teaspoon five-spice powder
1 tablespoon peanut oil
1 shallot (25g), sliced thinly
1 clove garlic, crushed
100g snake beans, chopped coarsely
1 tablespoon mirin
¼ cup (50g) rinsed, drained sliced bamboo shoots
2 teaspoons sesame seeds, toasted

1 Combine pork, sauces and five-spice in small bowl.
2 Heat half the oil in wok; stir-fry pork mixture until browned and sticky. Remove from wok.
3 Heat remaining oil in wok; stir-fry shallot, garlic and beans until beans are tender. Return pork to wok with mirin and bamboo shoots; stir-fry until hot, season to taste. Serve topped with sesame seeds.
nutritional count per serving 31.5g total fat (6.8g saturated fat); 2445kJ (585 cal); 19g carbohydrate; 49.3g protein; 10.7g fibre

Use thinly sliced pork fillet instead of pork strips if you like. Pork mixture can be marinated for a few hours or overnight in the fridge.

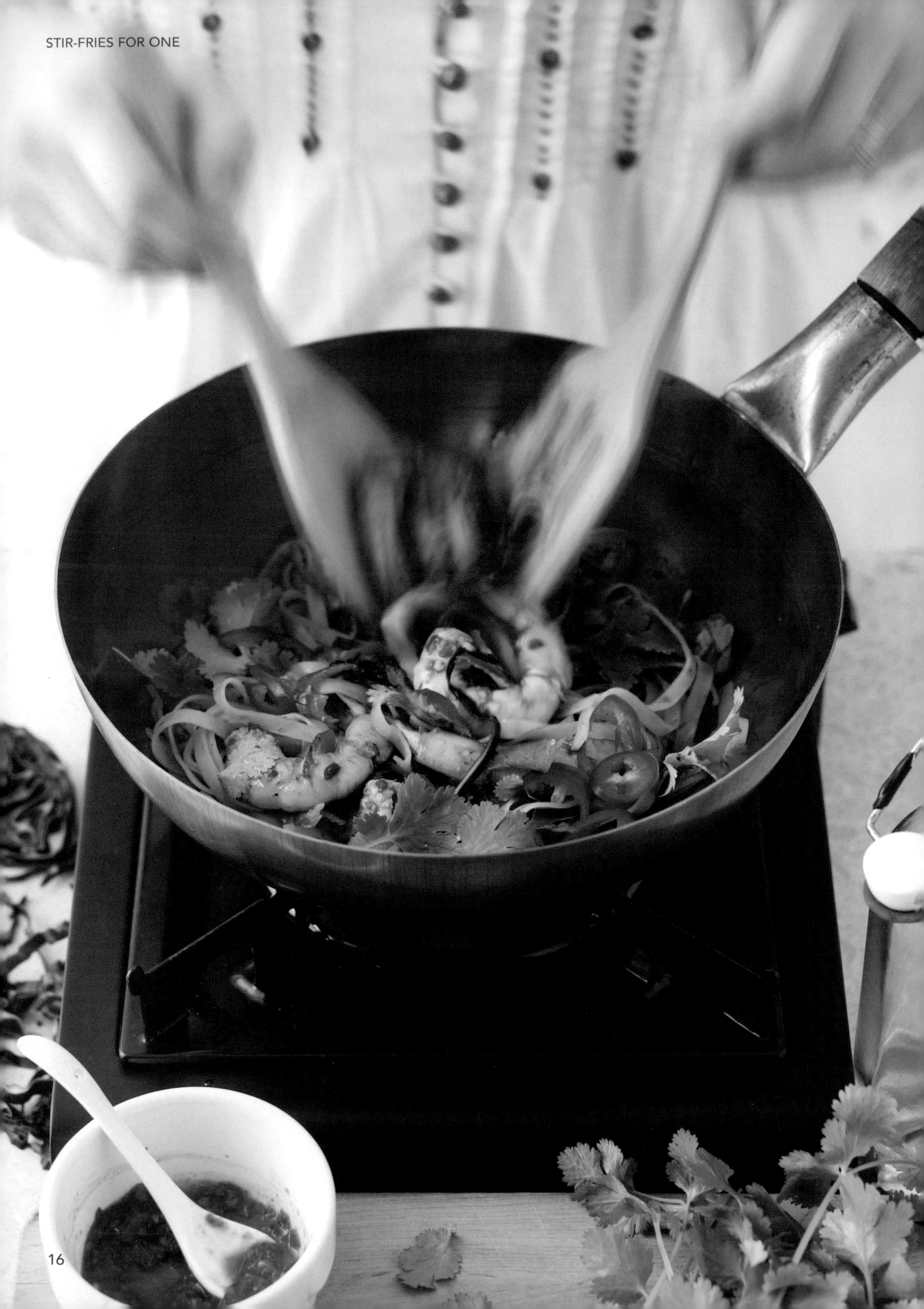

Hokkien noodles can be used instead of rice noodles.

Scallops or firm white fish fillets can be used instead of prawns. Prawn mixture can be marinated for a few hours or overnight in the fridge.

on the table in # 30 MIN

CHILLI PRAWNS WITH NOODLES

7 uncooked medium king prawns (300g)
1 clove garlic, crushed
2 tablespoons sambal oelek
2 teaspoons peanut oil
2 tablespoons finely chopped fresh coriander
100g dried rice stick noodles
2 teaspoons sesame oil
2 green onions, chopped finely
1 cup (80g) finely shredded red cabbage
2 teaspoons fish sauce
2 tablespoons oyster sauce
2 teaspoons brown sugar
1 fresh long red chilli, sliced thinly
¼ cup loosely packed fresh coriander leaves

1 Shell and devein prawns leaving tails intact; combine prawns, garlic, sambal, peanut oil and chopped coriander in small bowl, season.
2 Place noodles in medium heatproof bowl, cover with boiling water; stand until tender, drain.
3 Meanwhile, heat sesame oil in wok; stir-fry prawn mixture until prawns change colour.
4 Add onion, cabbage, sauces, sugar and noodles; stir-fry until cabbage wilts. Serve topped with chilli and coriander leaves.

nutritional count per serving 21.7g total fat (3.4g saturated fat); 2362kJ (565 cal); 50.2g carbohydrate; 37.9g protein; 7g fibre

on the table in **30 MIN**

INDONESIAN CHILLI LAMB WITH NOODLES

180g lamb strips
2 tablespoons oyster sauce
1 tablespoon sweet chilli sauce
1 clove garlic, crushed
1 tablespoon finely chopped fresh basil
150g hokkien noodles
1 tablespoon peanut oil
1 spring onion (25g), sliced thinly
50g oyster mushrooms, chopped coarsely
50g snow peas, trimmed

1   Combine lamb, sauces, garlic and basil in small bowl.
2   Place noodles in medium heatproof bowl, cover with boiling water; separate with fork, drain.
3   Heat half the oil in wok; stir-fry lamb mixture until browned. Remove from wok.
4   Heat remaining oil in wok; stir-fry onion until onion softens. Return lamb to wok with noodles, mushrooms and snow peas; stir-fry until hot, season to taste. Serve sprinkled with extra fresh basil leaves.
nutritional count per serving 28.9g total fat (6.5g saturated fat); 2976kJ (712 cal); 56.1g carbohydrate; 52.2g protein; 7.8g fibre

Lamb mixture can be marinated for a few hours or overnight in the fridge.

on the table in # 30 MIN

CITRUS FISH WITH GAI LAN

200g firm white fish fillets, cut into 3cm pieces
2 teaspoon finely grated lime rind
2 teaspoon finely grated lemon rind
2 teaspoons sweet chilli sauce
2 teaspoons fish sauce
1 teaspoon finely chopped fresh lemon grass
1 fresh kaffir lime leaf, shredded finely
1 tablespoon peanut oil
1 green onion, sliced thinly
2 tablespoons hoisin sauce
300g gai lan, trimmed, shredded finely
½ cup (100g) rinsed, drained sliced bamboo shoots

1 Combine fish, rinds, sweet chilli and fish sauces, lemon grass and lime leaf in small bowl.
2 Heat half the oil in wok; stir-fry fish until cooked. Remove from wok.
3 Heat remaining oil in wok; stir-fry onion until soft. Add hoisin sauce, gai lan and bamboo shoots; stir-fry until gai lan wilts. Return fish to wok; stir-fry until hot, season to taste.

nutritional count per serving 26.2g total fat (5.1g saturated fat); 2240kJ (536 cal); 22.6g carbohydrate; 47.1g protein; 12.4g fibre

We used blue-eye fillets in this recipe, but you can use any firm white fish fillets. Fish mixture can be marinated for 30 minutes. Serve with steamed jasmine rice and lemon or lime wedges.

FRIED RICE WITH CHILLI PASTE

on the table in 25 min

Whisk 1 egg with 1 teaspoon fish sauce in small bowl. Pour egg into heated oiled wok; cook omelette, tilting wok, until almost set. Remove omelette from wok; roll tightly then slice thinly. Heat oiled wok; stir-fry 1 thinly sliced garlic clove, 2 tablespoons chilli paste and 1 coarsely chopped baby pak choy until pak choy wilts. Add 1 cup cooked white long-grain rice; stir-fry until hot, season to taste. Serve fried rice topped with omelette and 1 thinly sliced green onion.

nutritional count per serving
25.8g total fat (4.7g saturated fat); 2132kJ (510 cal); 53.4g carbohydrate; 14.1g protein; 4.4g fibre

SALT AND PEPPER CHICKEN

on the table in 30 min

Combine 200g coarsely chopped chicken tenderloins, 2 teaspoons sea salt and 1 tablespoon lemon pepper in small bowl. Heat oiled wok; stir-fry chicken until cooked. Add 1 coarsely chopped pak choy and 1 tablespoon yellow miso paste; stir-fry until pak choy wilts. Add 1 cup cooked white long-grain rice; stir-fry until hot, season to taste. Serve fried rice topped with a few fresh thai basil leaves.

nutritional count per serving
17.2g total fat (4.2g saturated fat); 2500kJ (598 cal); 54.8g carbohydrate; 21.7g protein; 5.9g fibre

GARLIC GINGER RICE WITH CAJUN FISH

on the table in 20 min

Rub 200g firm white fish fillet all over with 1 tablespoon cajun spice mix. Heat oiled wok; cook fish, skin-side down, about 5 minutes or until skin is crisp. Turn fish; cook about 5 minutes. Remove fish from wok; cover to keep warm. Stir-fry 1 thinly sliced garlic clove and 1cm piece of finely sliced fresh ginger in heated oiled wok until fragrant. Add 1 cup cooked white long-grain rice, 1 thinly sliced green onion and 1 tablespoon cajun spice mix; stir-fry until hot, season to taste. Serve fried rice topped with fish, a handful of fresh coriander leaves and a dollop of yogurt.

nutritional count per serving
9g total fat (2g saturated fat); 1914kJ (458 cal); 47.6g carbohydrate; 45g protein; 1.4g fibre

We used a pink snapper fillet with the skin on. You could also use chicken or prawns instead of the fish.

WILD RICE WITH FENNEL

on the table in 30 min

Heat oiled wok; stir-fry ½ cup (80g) finely chopped pumpkin until almost tender. Add ½ thinly sliced small leek, 1 thinly sliced baby fennel bulb and 2 tablespoons pesto; stir-fry until vegetables are tender. Add 1 cup cooked wild rice; stir-fry until hot, season to taste. Serve fried rice sprinkled with 1 tablespoon crumbled fetta cheese.
nutritional count per serving
25.5g total fat (7.4g saturated fat); 1914kJ (458 cal); 36.9g carbohydrate; 16.5g protein; 8.2g fibre

We used store-bought basil pesto for this recipe. Arborio rice (or any short-grain rice) could be used instead of the wild rice.

FRIED RICE WITH SWEET BEEF

on the table in 30 min

Combine 150g beef strips and 1 tablespoon kecap manis in small bowl. Heat oiled wok; stir-fry beef until browned. Add 1 tablespoon yellow bean paste, 100g thinly sliced sugar snap peas and 1 cup cooked brown long-grain rice; stir-fry until hot, season to taste. Serve fried rice sprinkled with 1 tablespoon fried shallots.
nutritional count per serving
10.8g total fat (2.4g saturated fat); 2491kJ (596 cal); 97.2g carbohydrate; 52.9g protein; 6.8g fibre

NASI GORENG

on the table in 20 min

Heat oiled small frying pan; fry 1 egg, one side only, until barely set. Meanwhile, heat oiled wok; stir-fry 1 coarsely chopped rindless bacon rasher until browned. Add 1 tablespoon nasi goreng spice mix, 2 thinly sliced green onions and 1 cup cooked white long-grain rice; stir-fry until hot. Remove from heat; stir in 1 coarsely chopped seeded medium tomato, season to taste. Serve fried rice topped with egg; sprinkle with a little thinly sliced green onion.
nutritional count per serving
19.3g total fat (5.7g saturated fat); 2031kJ (486 cal); 50.7g carbohydrate; 25.7g protein; 2.8g fibre

Nasi goreng spice mix is available from Asian grocery stores and the Asian section of larger supermarkets.

STIR-FRIES FOR TWO

on the table in 25 MIN

THAI COCONUT AND CORIANDER PORK

½ cup (125ml) coconut milk
1 tablespoon coarsely chopped fresh coriander
  root and stem mixture
1 clove garlic, quartered
1 teaspoon fish sauce
250g pork fillet, sliced thinly
2 tablespoons peanut oil
2cm piece fresh ginger (10g), cut into matchsticks
500g baby pak choy, leaves separated
2 teaspoons lime juice
¼ cup loosely packed fresh coriander leaves
1 long green chilli, sliced thinly

1 Blend or process ⅓ cup of the coconut milk, coriander root and stem mixture, garlic and sauce until smooth; combine with pork in medium bowl.
2 Heat half the oil in wok; stir-fry ginger until fragrant. Add pak choy; stir-fry until pak choy is wilted. Remove from wok; cover to keep warm.
3 Drain pork; reserve marinade. Heat remaining oil in wok; stir-fry pork, in batches, until browned.
4 Add reserved marinade, remaining coconut milk and juice; bring to the boil. Return pork to wok; stir-fry until hot, season to taste.
5 Serve pak choy topped with pork mixture; sprinkle with coriander leaves and chilli.
nutritional count per serving 33.1g total fat (15.2g saturated fat); 1910kJ (457 cal); 5.6g carbohydrate; 32.3g protein; 5g fibre

Serve with lime wedges and steamed jasmine rice or noodles.
Use light coconut milk for a lower-fat version.

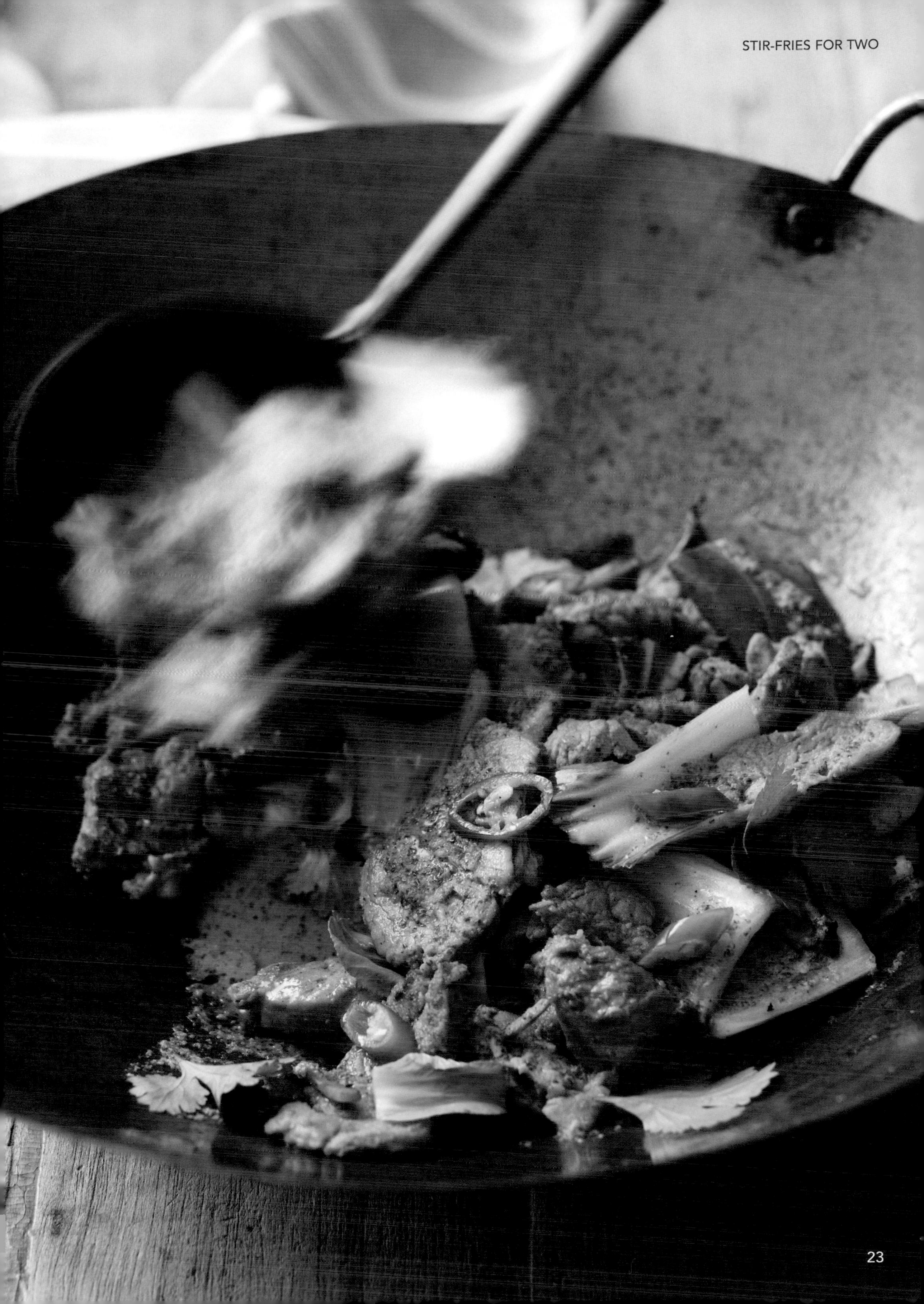

on the table in # 30 MIN

CURRIED MEATBALLS WITH GREEN BEANS AND WOMBOK

250g beef mince
2 teaspoons yellow curry paste
⅓ cup coarsely chopped fresh coriander
2 tablespoons peanut oil
1 medium brown onion (150g), sliced thinly
100g green beans, trimmed, halved
1 clove garlic, crushed
1 long green chilli, sliced thinly
1 teaspoon curry powder
½ small wombok (350g), shredded coarsely
2 tablespoons coconut cream
¼ cup (60ml) water

1 Combine mince, paste and 1 tablespoon of the coriander in small bowl; roll level tablespoons of mixture into balls. Heat half the oil in wok; stir-fry meatballs, in batches, until cooked through.
2 Heat remaining oil in wok; stir-fry onion and beans until beans are tender. Add garlic, chilli and curry powder; stir-fry until fragrant. Return meatballs to wok with wombok, coconut cream and the water; stir-fry until wombok wilts, season to taste. Sprinkle with remaining coriander to serve.

nutritional count per serving 36g total fat (12.1g saturated fat); 2011kJ (481 cal); 8.8g carbohydrate; 28.4g protein; 6g fibre

Use light coconut cream for a lower-fat version. Serve with steamed jasmine rice.

on the table in # 20 MIN

SWEET CHILLI MUSSELS AND HOKKIEN NOODLES

440g thin hokkien noodles
2 tablespoons peanut oil
1 shallot (25g), sliced thinly
2 cloves garlic, crushed
4cm piece fresh ginger (20g), grated
1kg mussels
2 tablespoons chinese cooking wine
2 green onions, sliced thinly
1 fresh long red chilli, sliced thinly
2 tablespoons sweet chilli sauce
¼ cup loosely packed fresh coriander leaves

1   Place noodles in medium heatproof bowl, cover with boiling water; separate with fork, drain.
2   Heat half the oil in wok; stir-fry shallot, garlic and ginger until shallot softens. Add mussels and cooking wine; cook, covered, about 5 minutes or until mussels open (discard any that do not). Remove mussels from wok, reserve ¼ cup cooking liquid. Remove half of the mussels from their shells.
3   Heat remaining oil in wok; stir-fry onion and chilli until onion softens. Return mussels to wok with noodles, sauce and reserved cooking liquid; stir-fry until hot, season to taste. Serve stir-fry sprinkled with coriander.
nutritional count per serving 22g total fat (4.2g saturated fat); 2454kJ (587 cal); 66.7g carbohydrate; 24.4g protein; 5.9g fibre

on the table in # 25 MIN

MONGOLIAN LAMB

250g lamb fillet, sliced thinly
2 teaspoons light soy sauce
2 teaspoons cornflour
2cm piece fresh ginger (10g), grated
1 clove garlic, crushed
1 tablespoon mirin
½ teaspoon sesame oil
1 tablespoon peanut oil
1 small brown onion (80g), cut into wedges
1 small red capsicum (150g), sliced thinly
1 tablespoon hoisin sauce
2 teaspoons oyster sauce
1 tablespoon water
100g snow peas, trimmed
1 fresh small red thai chilli, chopped finely
2 green onions, sliced thinly

1 Combine lamb, soy sauce, cornflour, ginger, garlic, mirin and sesame oil in small bowl.
2 Heat half the peanut oil in wok; stir-fry lamb mixture, in batches, until browned. Remove from wok.
3 Heat remaining oil in wok; stir-fry brown onion and capsicum until tender. Return lamb to wok with sauces, the water and peas; stir-fry until hot. Remove from heat; stir in chilli and half the green onion, season to taste. Serve sprinkled with remaining green onion.

nutritional count per serving 16.5g total fat (3.7g saturated fat); 1459kJ (349 cal); 15.4g carbohydrate; 31.4g protein; 4g fibre

Serve with steamed jasmine rice or noodles. Lamb mixture can be marinated for 3 hours or overnight in the fridge.

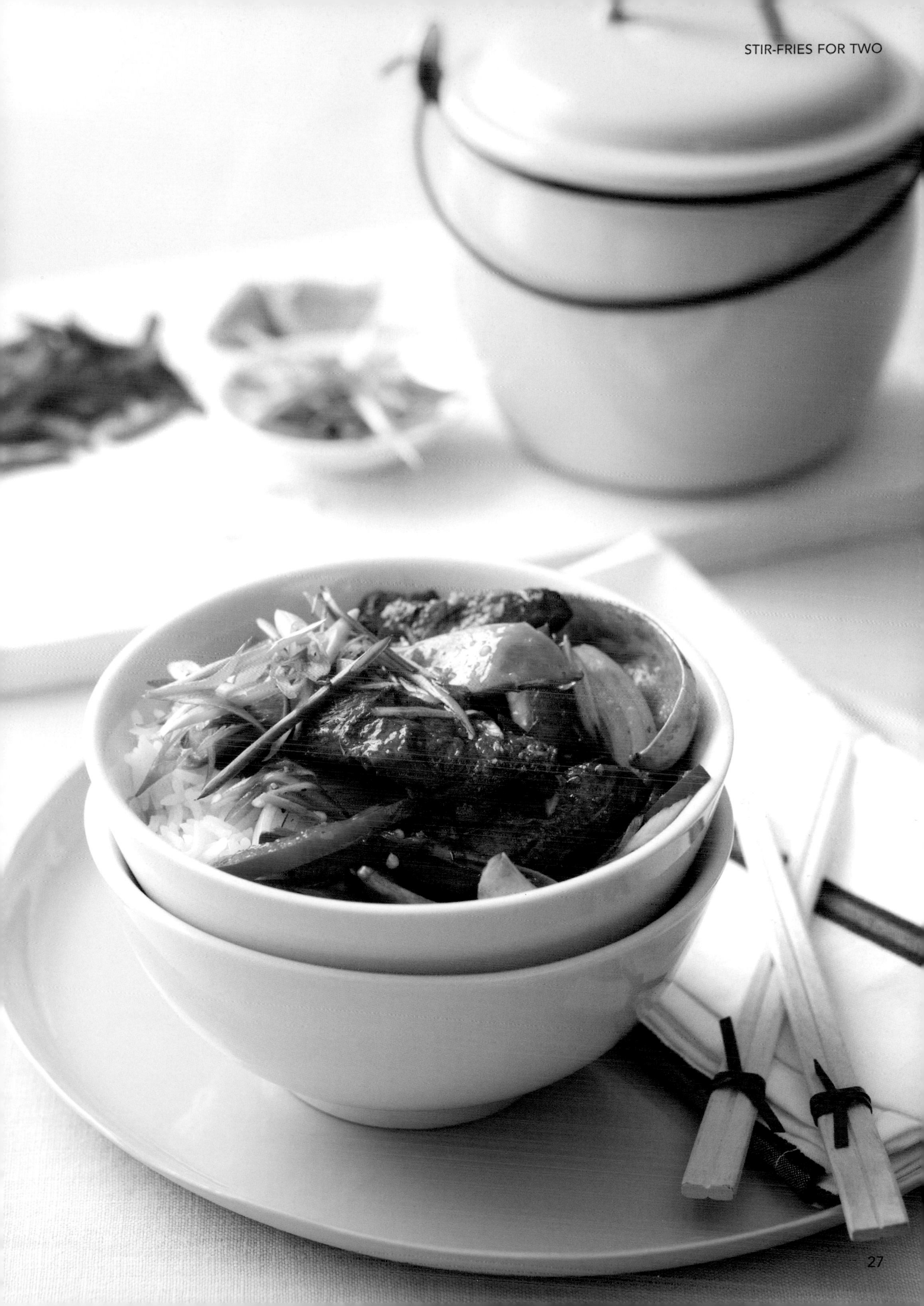

on the table in # 25 MIN

THAI RED CHICKEN CURRY

1½ tablespoons peanut oil
200g pumpkin, cut into 2cm pieces
2 baby eggplants (120g), halved lengthways,
 chopped coarsely
250g chicken thigh fillets, sliced thinly
270ml can coconut milk
⅓ cup (80ml) water
2 tablespoons lime juice
1 tablespoon red curry paste
1 fresh kaffir lime leaf, shredded finely
2 teaspoons fish sauce
1 tablespoon small thai basil leaves

1 Heat 1 tablespoon of the oil in wok; stir-fry pumpkin and eggplant until browned lightly and almost tender. Remove from wok.
2 Heat remaining oil in wok; stir-fry chicken, in batches, until browned.
3 Return chicken, pumpkin and eggplant to wok with coconut milk, the water, juice, paste, lime leaf and sauce; simmer, uncovered, until chicken is cooked through and vegetables are tender, season to taste. Serve curry sprinkled with basil.
nutritional count per serving 52g total fat (29.5g saturated fat); 2696kJ (645 cal); 13.3g carbohydrate; 29.1g protein; 6g fibre

Serve with steamed jasmine rice. Use light coconut milk, if you prefer.

on the table in # 20 MIN

FIVE-SPICE FISH WITH GREENS

2 tablespoons plain flour
3 teaspoons five-spice powder
250g firm white fish fillets, cut into 3cm pieces
2 tablespoons peanut oil
175g broccolini, cut into 3cm lengths
1 clove garlic, crushed
150g snow peas, trimmed
2 tablespoons water
1 tablespoon japanese soy sauce
1 fresh long red chilli, sliced thinly

1 Combine flour and five-spice in small shallow bowl; toss fish in flour mixture to coat. Heat half the oil in wok; stir-fry fish, in batches, until browned lightly. Remove from wok.
2 Heat remaining oil in wok; stir-fry broccolini and garlic until fragrant. Add peas, the water and sauce; stir-fry until broccolini is tender. Return fish to wok with chilli; stir-fry until hot, season to taste.
nutritional count per serving 21.6g total fat (4.2g saturated fat); 1647kJ (394 cal); 13g carbohydrate; 34g protein; 6.4g fibre

We used blue-eye fillets in this recipe, but you can use any white fish fillets.

This recipe is traditionally known as mu shu pork. Peking duck pancakes are small, round crêpes or pancakes made with plain flour; they can be purchased commercially from Asian food stores.

on the table in ## 25 MIN

PORK AND VEGIE PANCAKES

12 peking duck pancakes (230g)
1 tablespoon peanut oil
250g pork mince
1 tablespoon chinese cooking wine
1 tablespoon japanese soy sauce
1 tablespoon oyster sauce
1 small carrot (70g), cut into matchsticks
100g fresh shiitake mushrooms, sliced thinly
½ x 225g can sliced bamboo shoots,
   rinsed, drained
4 green onions, sliced thinly
1 teaspoon sesame oil

1 Heat pancakes by folding each into quarters, place in steamer over large pan of simmering water; steam until warm and pliable.
2 Meanwhile, heat half the peanut oil in wok; stir-fry mince until browned. Remove mince from wok; combine in medium bowl with cooking wine and sauces.
3 Heat remaining peanut oil in wok; stir-fry carrot and mushrooms until tender. Return mince mixture to wok with bamboo shoots and half the green onion; stir-fry until liquid is almost evaporated. Remove from heat; stir in sesame oil, season to taste.
4 Serve mince mixture with pancakes; sprinkle with remaining green onion.
nutritional count per serving 26.9g total fat (8.1g saturated fat); 2224kJ (532 cal); 32.7g carbohydrate; 36.4g protein; 4.4g fibre

on the table in # 20 MIN

SQUID CURRY NOODLES

350g chow mein noodles
250g cleaned squid hoods
1 clove garlic, crushed
1 tablespoon japanese soy sauce
1 tablespoon peanut oil
1 small brown onion (80g), sliced thinly
150g green beans, trimmed, halved
1 teaspoon curry powder
1/3 cup (80ml) coconut cream
1 tablespoon lime juice
2 tablespoons fresh coriander leaves

1 Place noodles in medium heatproof bowl, cover with boiling water; stand until tender, drain.
2 Meanwhile, cut squid down centre to open out; score inside in diagonal pattern then cut squid into thick strips.
3 Combine squid, garlic and sauce in small bowl. Heat half the oil in wok. Stir-fry squid mixture, in batches, until cooked. Remove from wok.
4 Heat remaining oil in wok; stir-fry onion and beans until beans are tender. Add curry powder; stir-fry until fragrant. Return squid to wok with noodles, coconut cream and juice; stir-fry until hot, season to taste. Serve sprinkled with coriander.
nutritional count per serving 21.2g total fat (9.8g saturated fat); 3185kJ (732 cal); 96.7g carbohydrate; 41.2g protein; 7.1g fibre

Use light coconut cream, if you prefer.

on the table in 20 MIN

BEEF AND BLACK BEAN

1 tablespoon peanut oil
250g beef rump steak, sliced thinly
1 small brown onion (80g), cut into wedges
1 small yellow capsicum (150g), chopped coarsely
400g choy sum, stems and leaves separated,
  chopped coarsely
1½ tablespoons spicy black bean sauce
2 teaspoons japanese soy sauce
227g can whole water chestnuts, rinsed,
  drained, quartered
1 tablespoon water
2 tablespoons coarsely chopped roasted
  macadamia nuts

1 Heat half the oil in wok; stir-fry beef, in batches, until browned. Remove from wok.
2 Heat remaining oil in wok; stir-fry onion, capsicum and choy sum stalks until stalks are tender. Add choy sum leaves; stir-fry until wilted.
3 Return beef to wok with sauces, chestnuts and the water; stir fry until hot, season to taste. Serve sprinkled with nuts.
nutritional count per serving 21.2g total fat (4.5g saturated fat); 1634kJ (391 cal); 15.9g carbohydrate; 31.3g protein; 6.9g fibre

Spicy black bean sauce is available from Asian grocery stores and the Asian section of larger supermarkets. You can use a milder black bean sauce, if you prefer.

on the table in # 20 MIN

PRAWNS AND PORK WITH RICE NOODLES

4 uncooked medium king prawns (180g)
250g fresh wide rice noodles
2 dried chinese sausages (60g), sliced thinly
1 tablespoon peanut oil
100g pork fillet, sliced thinly
2 cloves garlic, crushed
1 fresh small red thai chilli, chopped finely
1 tablespoon dark soy sauce
2 teaspoons light soy sauce
1 egg
2 tablespoons coarsely chopped
  fresh garlic chives

1 Shell and devein prawns leaving tails intact.
2 Place noodles in medium heatproof bowl, cover with boiling water; separate with fork, drain.
3 Heat wok; stir-fry sausage until crisp; drain on absorbent paper.
4 Heat oil in wok; stir-fry pork, garlic and chilli until pork is browned. Add prawns; stir-fry until prawns change colour. Return sausage to wok with noodles and sauces; stir-fry until hot.
5 Make a well in centre of noodles. Add egg; stir-fry until egg and noodle mixture is combined, season to taste. Serve noodles sprinkled with chives.
nutritional count per serving 21.3g total fat (5.4g saturated fat); 1822kJ (436 cal); 28.5g carbohydrate; 31.3g protein; 2.2g fibre

Traditionally this recipe is known as char kway teow.

Dried chinese sausages, also called lop chong, are usually made from pork. They are red-brown in colour and sweet-spicy in flavour. They are available in all Asian grocery stores.

on the table in **15 MIN**

STIR-FRIED PRAWN OMELETTE

300g uncooked medium king prawns
1 tablespoon peanut oil
4 eggs, beaten lightly
4 green onions, cut into 6cm lengths
1 clove garlic, chopped finely
2cm piece fresh ginger (10g), grated
¼ cup (60ml) chicken stock
1 teaspoon japanese soy sauce
1 cup (80g) bean sprouts

1 Shell and devein prawns; leaving tails intact.
2 Heat half the oil in wok. Pour egg into wok; cook omelette, tilting wok, until almost set. Remove omelette from wok; cover to keep warm.
3 Heat remaining oil in wok; stir-fry prawns, onion, garlic and ginger until prawns change colour.
4 Add stock and sauce to wok; bring to the boil. Return omelette to wok; stir fry until hot, breaking omelette into pieces, season to taste. Remove from heat; stir in sprouts.

nutritional count per serving 21.7g total fat (5.5g saturated fat); 1392kJ (333 cal); 1.7g carbohydrate; 32.4g protein; 1.6g fibre

on the table in # 20 MIN

CHILLI BEAN CHICKEN

250g chicken thigh fillets, chopped coarsely
1 tablespoon japanese soy sauce
1 tablespoon chinese cooking wine
1 teaspoon sesame oil
1 tablespoon peanut oil
2 green onions, sliced thinly
2cm piece fresh ginger (10g), grated
1 clove garlic, crushed
1 tablespoon chilli bean paste
300g spinach, chopped coarsely
½ teaspoon sichuan peppercorns,
  crushed coarsely

1 Combine chicken with half each of the soy sauce, cooking wine and sesame oil in small bowl. Drain chicken; reserve marinade.

2 Heat half the peanut oil in wok; stir-fry chicken, in batches, until browned. Remove from wok.

3 Heat remaining peanut oil in wok; stir-fry onion, ginger and garlic until fragrant. Return chicken to wok with reserved marinade, paste, remaining sauce, wine and sesame oil; bring to the boil, stir-fry until chicken is cooked through. Add spinach; stir-fry until wilted. Serve sprinkled with pepper.

nutritional count per serving 18.3g total fat (3.9g saturated fat); 1229kJ (294 cal); 2.9g carbohydrate; 26.5g protein; 3.2g fibre

Traditionally this recipe is known as chengdu chicken. Serve it with steamed jasmine rice. The chicken mixture can be marinated for a few hours or overnight in the fridge.

on the table in # 25 MIN

COMBINATION SESAME NOODLE SALAD

200g uncooked medium king prawns
2½ tablespoons sesame seeds, toasted
2 tablespoons water
1 tablespoon smooth peanut butter
1 teaspoon brown malt vinegar
1 tablespoon japanese soy sauce
2 teaspoons chilli sauce
2 teaspoons sesame oil
125g dried egg noodles
1 lebanese cucumber (130g), seeded,
 cut into matchsticks
½ small red capsicum (75g), cut into matchsticks
2 green onions, sliced thinly
1 tablespoon peanut oil
150g chicken thigh fillets, sliced thinly

1 Shell and devein prawns.
2 Blend or crush 2 tablespoons of the seeds to a coarse powder; transfer to small bowl. Stir in the water, peanut butter, vinegar, sauces and sesame oil.
3 Cook noodles in medium saucepan of boiling water until tender; drain. Rinse under cold water; drain. Combine noodles, cucumber, capsicum, onion and sesame seed mixture in medium bowl; season to taste.
4 Meanwhile, heat half the peanut oil in wok; stir-fry chicken, in batches, until cooked. Remove from wok.
5 Heat remaining oil in wok; stir-fry prawns until changed in colour.
6 Stir chicken and prawns through noodle mixture; sprinkle with remaining seeds.
nutritional count per serving 33g total fat (5.7g saturated fat); 2776kJ (664 cal); 48.7g carbohydrate; 39.9g protein; 5.6g fibre

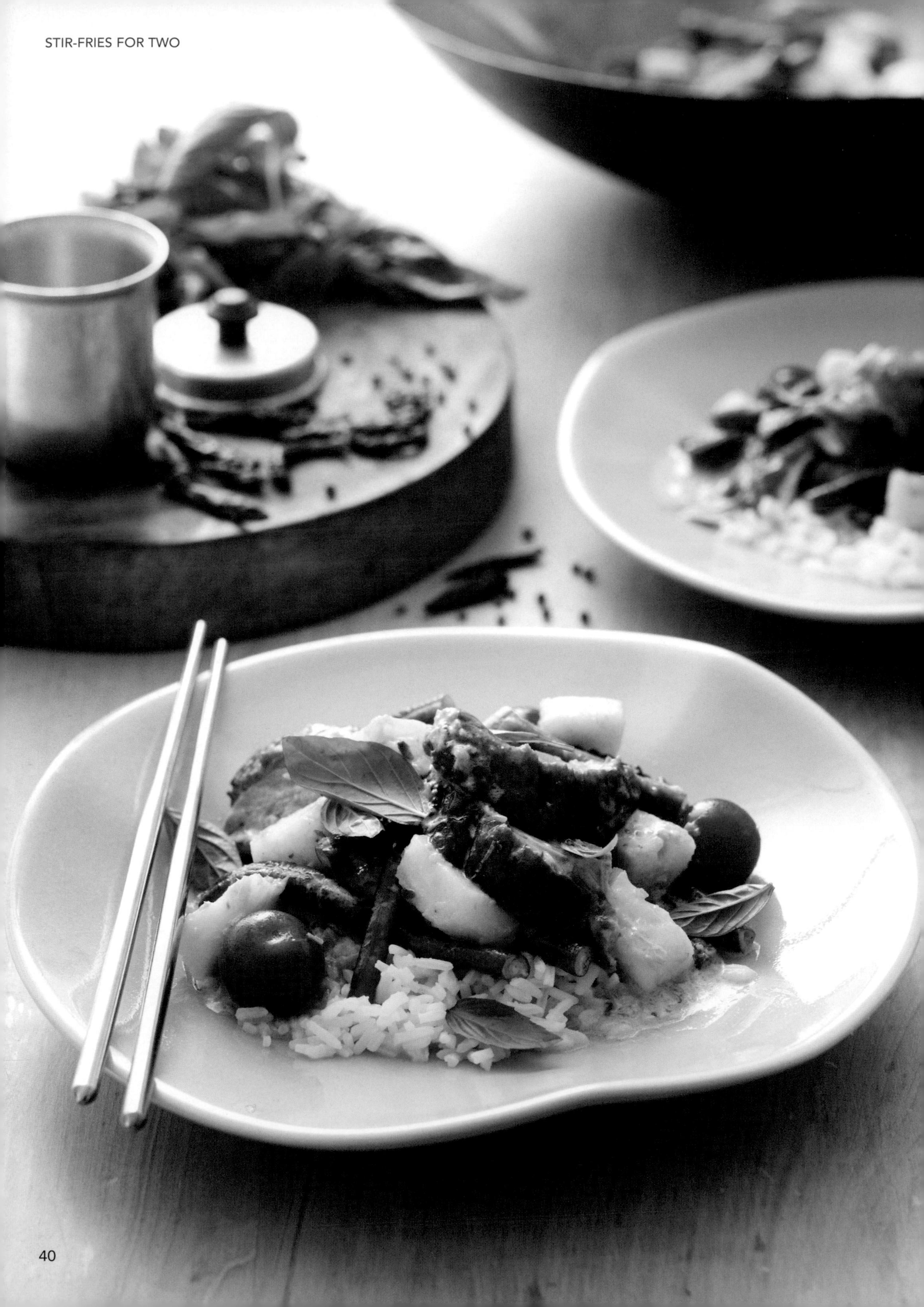

on the table in # 35 MIN

PANANG DUCK CURRY

½ chinese barbecued duck (500g)
150g snake beans, cut into 5cm lengths
270ml can coconut milk
½ cup (125ml) water
400g pineapple, peeled, cored, chopped coarsely
60g cherry tomatoes
1 tablespoon small thai basil leaves
PANANG CURRY PASTE
1 teaspoon coriander seeds
15 dried red chillies, seeded
6 cloves garlic, quartered
6 coriander roots
2 shallots (50g), chopped coarsely
2 x 10cm sticks fresh lemon grass (40g),
  sliced thinly
2 tablespoons coarsely chopped roasted
  unsalted peanuts
4cm piece fresh galangal (20g), grated
⅓ cup (80ml) water
1 tablespoon shrimp paste
1 tablespoon peanut oil

1 Make panang curry paste.
2 Quarter duck; discard bones. Slice duck meat thickly, keeping skin intact.
3 Heat oiled wok; stir-fry beans until tender. Add 2 tablespoons of the curry paste; stir-fry about 2 minutes or until fragrant. Add coconut milk, the water, pineapple and duck; simmer, uncovered, until heated through. Add tomatoes; season to taste. Serve sprinkled with thai basil.
panang curry paste Dry-fry seeds in heated small frying pan until fragrant. Blend or process seeds with remaining ingredients until smooth, season to taste.
nutritional count per serving 80g total fat (38g saturated fat); 4046kJ (968 cal); 22.2g carbohydrate; 37.5g protein; 9.9g fibre

Serve with steamed jasmine rice.
This recipe makes 1 cup panang curry paste. Store leftover curry paste, covered, in the fridge for up to three days, or freeze in user-friendly portions for up to three months. Use a bought panang curry paste, if you prefer.
Gently squeeze and shake the dried chillies to remove the seeds.

SALT AND PEPPER BEEF WITH LIME

on the table in 15 min

Season 2 tablespoons plain flour with salt and pepper in small bowl. Toss 250g thinly sliced beef rump steak in flour to coat; shake off excess. Heat vegetable oil for deep-frying in wok; deep-fry beef, in batches, until browned lightly. Drain on absorbent paper. Reheat 1 reserved tablespoon of the oil in wok; stir-fry 2 thinly sliced fresh long red chillies until fragrant. Return beef to wok; stir-fry until hot. Serve beef with lime wedges; sprinkle with 2 tablespoons fresh coriander leaves.

nutritional count per serving
22.1g total fat (4.2g saturated fat); 1430kJ (342 cal); 8.9g carbohydrate; 27g protein; 1.2g fibre

Serve beef with steamed rice or noodles.

DUCK BREASTS WITH GREEN ONION SAUCE

on the table in 25 min

Heat 1 tablespoon peanut oil in wok; stir-fry 3 thinly sliced green onions and 4cm piece grated fresh ginger until onion softens. Remove from wok; season to taste. Cook 2 duck breasts, skin-side down, in cleaned heated, oiled wok about 5 minutes or until skin is crisp. Turn duck; cook about 5 minutes or until cooked, reserve pan drippings. Cover duck; stand 5 minutes then slice thinly. Meanwhile, cut 2 trimmed celery stalks and 1 medium carrot into matchsticks. Reheat 1 tablespoon reserved pan drippings in wok; stir-fry celery and carrot until tender. Serve vegetables topped with duck and green onion sauce.

nutritional count per serving
58.8g total fat (18.8g saturated fat); 2805kJ (671 cal); 5.2g carbohydrate; 30.7g protein; 3.4g fibre

Serve with steamed rice.

CHILLI GARLIC SPINACH

on the table in 10 min

Cut 1 fresh long red chilli into matchsticks. Trim and coarsely chop 600g spinach. Heat oiled wok; stir-fry chilli and 1 finely chopped garlic clove until fragrant. Add spinach; stir-fry until spinach wilts. Add 1 tablespoon coconut cream, 1 tablespoon lime juice and ½ teaspoon shrimp paste; stir-fry until hot, season to taste.

nutritional count per serving
7.3g total fat (2.4g saturated fat); 435kJ (104 cal); 2.5g carbohydrate; 4.5g protein; 5.1g fibre

Serve as an accompaniment to meat or chicken, with steamed jasmine rice.
Omit the shrimp paste to make this dish suitable for vegetarians.

SINGAPORE PRAWNS WITH NOODLES

on the table in 20 min

Place 220g singapore noodles in medium heatproof bowl, cover with boiling water; separate with fork, drain. Meanwhile, shell and devein 12 uncooked medium king prawns, leaving tails intact. Heat oiled wok; stir-fry 2 thinly sliced shallots until browned lightly. Add 200ml can singapore hot curry sauce; bring to the boil. Reduce heat; simmer, uncovered, until sauce thickens slightly. Add prawns; simmer, uncovered, until prawns change colour. Add noodles and 1 tablespoon lime juice; stir-fry until hot, season to taste. Serve noodles sprinkled with 2 thinly sliced green onions.
nutritional count per serving
19.3g total fat (8.3g saturated fat); 1986kJ (475 cal); 36.4g carbohydrate; 35.4g protein; 3.9g fibre

CURRIED LAMB WITH CAPSICUM

on the table in 20 min

Cut 1 small brown onion into wedges. Coarsely chop 1 small red and 1 small yellow capsicum. Heat oiled wok; stir-fry 250g thinly sliced lamb fillet, in batches, until browned. Remove lamb from wok. Reheat oiled wok; stir fry onion and capsicum until tender. Return lamb to wok with 2 teaspoons sambal oelek, ½ teaspoon curry powder, 10 small fresh curry leaves and 2 tablespoons water; stir-fry until hot, season to taste.
nutritional count per serving
12g total fat (3.5g saturated fat); 1095kJ (292 cal); 8.3g carbohydrate; 29.2g protein; 2.3g fibre

Serve with steamed rice.

SPICY STIR-FRIED SQUID SALAD

on the table in 20 min

Cut 250g cleaned squid hoods down centre to open out; score inside in diagonal pattern then cut into 4cm pieces. Heat oiled wok; stir-fry 250g coarsely shredded wombok until wilted, remove from wok. Reheat oiled wok; stir-fry squid and 1 tablespoon chilli and garlic paste until squid is tender. Remove from heat; stir in 2 tablespoons lime juice, season to taste. Combine squid, wombok and ²/₃ cup each of loosely packed fresh mint and coriander leaves.
nutritional count per serving
6.6g total fat (1.4g saturated fat); 744kJ (178 cal); 4.2g carbohydrate; 23.1g protein; 3.2g fibre

STIR-FRIES FOR FAMILIES

on the table in **25 MIN** serves **4**

CHICKEN PAD THAI

500g fresh wide rice noodles
1 tablespoon peanut oil
2 eggs, beaten lightly
500g chicken breast fillets, sliced thinly
1 medium brown onion (150g), sliced thinly
3 cloves garlic, crushed
2 tablespoons lime juice
2 tablespoons fish sauce
1 tablespoon brown sugar
1 cup (80g) bean sprouts
3 green onions, sliced thinly
½ cup coarsely chopped fresh coriander
¼ cup (35g) roasted unsalted peanuts,
  chopped coarsely

1 Place noodles in large heatproof bowl, cover with boiling water; separate with fork, drain.
2 Heat 1 teaspoon of the oil in wok. Pour egg into wok; cook omelette, tilting wok, until omelette is barely set. Remove omelette from wok; roll tightly then slice thinly.
3 Heat 2 teaspoons of the remaining oil in wok; stir-fry chicken, in batches, until browned. Remove from wok.
4 Heat remaining oil in wok; stir-fry brown onion and garlic until onion softens. Return chicken to wok with noodles, juice, sauce and sugar; stir-fry until hot. Remove from heat; stir in sprouts, green onion and half the coriander, season to taste.
5 Serve noodles topped with omelette, nuts and remaining coriander.
nutritional count per serving 14.3g total fat (2.9g saturated fat); 1789kJ (428 cal); 34.1g carbohydrate; 38.6g protein; 3g fibre

on the table in **20 MIN** serves 4

FRIED RICE WITH TOMATO, PINEAPPLE AND SNOW PEAS

1 tablespoon peanut oil
200g snow peas, trimmed, sliced thickly
4 green onions, sliced thinly
2 cloves garlic, crushed
4 cups cooked white long-grain rice
¼ cup (60ml) japanese soy sauce
1 tablespoon fish sauce
1 tablespoon lime juice
500g pineapple, peeled, cored,
  cut into 1cm pieces
2 medium tomatoes (300g), seeded,
  cut into 1cm pieces
½ cup loosely packed fresh coriander leaves

1 Heat oil in wok; stir-fry snow peas, onion and garlic until snow peas are tender. Add rice, sauces and juice; stir-fry until hot. Remove from heat; stir in pineapple and tomato, season to taste.
2 Serve fried rice sprinkled with coriander.
nutritional count per serving 5.4g total fat (0.8g saturated fat); 1354kJ (324 cal); 57.1g carbohydrate; 8.4g protein; 4.7g fibre

You need to cook about 1⅓ cups white long-grain rice the day before making this recipe. Spread it evenly onto a tray and refrigerate overnight.

on the table in **30 MIN** serves **4**

CHOPPED NOODLES WITH LAMB

660g fresh udon noodles
600g lamb fillet, cut into 1cm pieces
2 tablespoons japanese soy sauce
1½ tablespoons peanut oil
1 small red capsicum (150g), sliced thinly
1 stalk celery (150g), trimmed, sliced thinly
½ small wombok (350g), shredded finely
3 green onions, sliced thinly
1 clove garlic, crushed
4cm piece fresh ginger (20g), grated
¼ cup (60ml) chinese black vinegar
1 large tomato (220g), sliced finely

1 Place noodles in large heatproof bowl, cover with boiling water; separate with fork, drain. Using scissors, cut noodles into 2cm pieces.
2 Combine lamb and half the sauce in medium bowl. Heat 1 tablespoon of the oil in wok; stir-fry lamb, in batches, until browned. Remove from wok.
3 Heat remaining oil in wok; stir-fry capsicum and celery until vegetables are tender. Add wombok, onion, garlic and ginger; stir-fry until wombok wilts. Return lamb to wok with noodles, vinegar and remaining sauce; stir-fry until hot. Remove from heat; stir in tomato, season to taste.

nutritional count per serving 15.9g total fat (4.4g saturated fat); 2087kJ (498 cal); 44.1g carbohydrate; 40.9g protein; 5.2g fibre

on the table in **20 MIN** serves **4**

SWEET AND SOY PORK

500g fresh wide rice noodles
1½ tablespoons peanut oil
500g pork fillet, sliced thinly
300g gai lan, chopped coarsely
3 cloves garlic, crushed
2 tablespoons light soy sauce
2 tablespoons dark soy sauce
2 tablespoons brown sugar
1 egg

1 Place noodles in large heatproof bowl, cover with boiling water; separate with fork, drain.
2 Heat 1 tablespoon of the oil in wok; stir-fry pork, in batches, until browned. Remove from wok.
3 Separate leaves and stems from gai lan. Heat remaining oil in wok; stir-fry gai lan stems until tender. Add gai lan leaves and garlic; stir-fry until gai lan wilts. Return pork to wok with noodles, sauces and sugar; stir-fry until hot.
4 Make a well in centre of noodles, add egg; stir-fry egg until egg and noodle mixture are combined, season to taste.
nutritional count per serving 12g total fat (2.7g saturated fat); 1622kJ (388 cal); 34.6g carbohydrate; 34g protein; 2.2g fibre

Traditionally, this recipe is known as pork pad see ew.

on the table in **25 MIN** serves **4**

UDON NOODLES WITH BEEF AND TOMATO

800g fresh udon noodles
2 tablespoons peanut oil
600g beef mince
2 tablespoons chinese cooking wine
4cm piece fresh ginger (20g), grated
2 cloves garlic, crushed
4 green onions, sliced thinly
⅓ cup (80ml) hoisin sauce
1 tablespoon japanese soy sauce
1 tablespoon tomato paste
1½ cups (325ml) chicken stock
2 large tomatoes (440g), seeded, sliced thinly
½ cup loosely packed fresh coriander leaves

1 Place noodles in large heatproof bowl, cover with boiling water; separate with fork, drain.
2 Heat half the oil in wok; stir-fry mince until browned. Add cooking wine; stir-fry until liquid has evaporated. Remove from wok.
3 Heat remaining oil in wok; stir-fry ginger, garlic and onion until fragrant. Return mince to wok with sauces, paste and stock; bring to the boil. Simmer, stirring occasionally, until sauce thickens slightly.
4 Add noodles and tomato; stir-fry until hot, season to taste. Serve noodles sprinkled with coriander.

nutritional count per serving 21.7g total fat (6.3g saturated fat); 2583kJ (618 cal); 59.9g carbohydrate; 40.8g protein; 6.9g fibre

Serve with steamed jasmine rice.
Try broccolini or broccoli instead of the asparagus.

on the table in **25 MIN** serves **4**

BEEF WITH ASPARAGUS AND OYSTER SAUCE

2 tablespoons peanut oil
500g beef rump steak, sliced thinly
1 medium brown onion (150g), cut into wedges
340g asparagus, trimmed, cut into 3cm lengths
2 cloves garlic, chopped finely
2 tablespoons oyster sauce
1 tablespoon japanese soy sauce

1   Heat half the oil in wok; stir-fry beef, in batches, until browned.

2   Heat remaining oil in wok; stir-fry onion until softened. Add asparagus; stir-fry until tender. Return beef to wok with garlic; stir-fry until fragrant. Add sauces; stir-fry until hot, season to taste. For extra heat, sprinkle with sliced fresh red chillies.

nutritional count per serving 15.1g total fat (3.8g saturated fat); 1166kJ (279 cal); 6.1g carbohydrate; 28.6g protein; 2g fibre

We used a combination of enoki, swiss brown and fresh shiitake mushrooms; you could also use button or oyster mushrooms.

on the table in **25 MIN** serves **4**

BEEF AND MUSHROOM OMELETTE

2 tablespoons peanut oil
400g beef rump steak, sliced thinly
250g mixed mushrooms, sliced thickly
4 green onions, sliced thinly
2 cloves garlic, crushed
2 tablespoons oyster sauce
8 eggs
2 tablespoons water
2 teaspoons japanese soy sauce
50g baby spinach leaves

1 Heat 2 teaspoons of the oil in wok; stir-fry beef, in batches, until browned. Remove from wok.
2 Heat 2 teaspoons of the remaining oil in wok; stir-fry mushrooms until browned lightly. Add onion and garlic; stir-fry until fragrant. Return beef to wok with oyster sauce; stir-fry until hot, season to taste. Remove from wok; cover to keep warm.
3 Whisk eggs with the water and soy sauce in large jug. Heat 1 teaspoon of the remaining oil in same cleaned wok; pour a quarter of egg mixture into wok, tilting wok to make a 20cm omelette, cook until almost set. Slide omelette onto serving plate; top with a quarter of the beef mixture and a quarter of the spinach. Fold omelette to enclose filling; cover to keep warm.
4 Repeat to make a total of four omelettes.
nutritional count per serving 26g total fat (7g saturated fat); 1705kJ (408 cal); 4.3g carbohydrate; 38.5g protein; 2.2g fibre

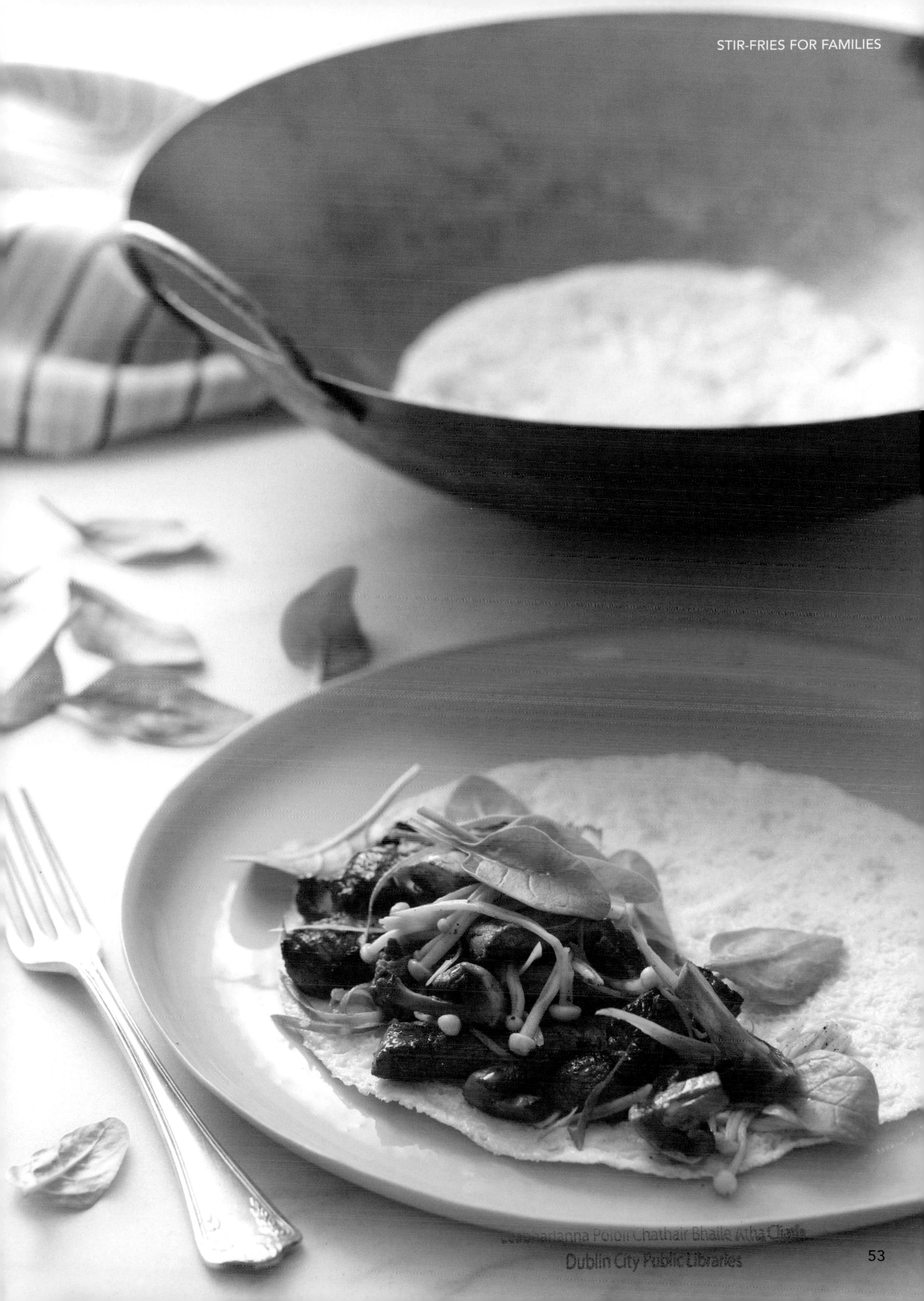

on the table in **25 MIN** serves **4**

FISH WITH MIXED VEGETABLES

2 cloves garlic, chopped finely
2½ tablespoons peanut oil
500g firm white fish fillets, cut into 3cm pieces
350g broccolini, cut into 3cm lengths
1 large carrot (180g), cut into matchsticks
150g baby corn, halved lengthways
¼ cup (60ml) oyster sauce
1 tablespoon japanese soy sauce
1 tablespoon water

1 Combine garlic, 2 tablespoons of the oil and fish in medium bowl. Heat wok; stir-fry fish, in batches, until browned. Remove from wok.
2 Heat remaining oil in wok; stir-fry broccolini, carrot and corn until vegetables are tender. Return fish to wok with sauces and the water; stir-fry until hot, season to taste.
nutritional count per serving 15.1g total fat (3g saturated fat); 1388kJ (332 cal); 12.9g carbohydrate; 32.4g protein; 6.7g fibre

**We used blue-eye fillets in this recipe, but you can use any white fish fillets.
Serve with steamed jasmine rice.**

on the table in **25 MIN** serves **4**

CARAMEL FISH AND BABY PAK CHOY

⅔ cup (150g) caster sugar
⅓ cup (80ml) fish sauce
4 shallots (100g), sliced thinly
1kg baby pak choy, leaves separated
2 tablespoons peanut oil
500g white fish fillets, cut into 3cm pieces

1   Heat sugar in medium saucepan over medium heat until sugar melts and turns a light caramel colour. Remove pan from heat; add sauce. Return pan to heat; simmer caramel sauce, stirring, until sauce becomes syrupy; stir in shallot.
2   Meanwhile, boil, steam or microwave pak choy until wilted; drain. Cover to keep warm.

3   Heat oil in wok. Stir-fry fish, in batches, until browned. Add caramel sauce; bring to the boil. Simmer, uncovered, until fish is cooked.
4   Divide pak choy between serving plates; top with fish, drizzle with sauce.

nutritional count per serving 12.5g total fat (2.5g saturated fat); 1676kJ (401 cal); 41.8g carbohydrate; 30.2g protein; 3.8g fibre

We used blue-eye fillets in this recipe, but you can use any white fish fillets.
Caramel sauce can be made in advance. Cover; refrigerate until required.
Serve with steamed jasmine rice.

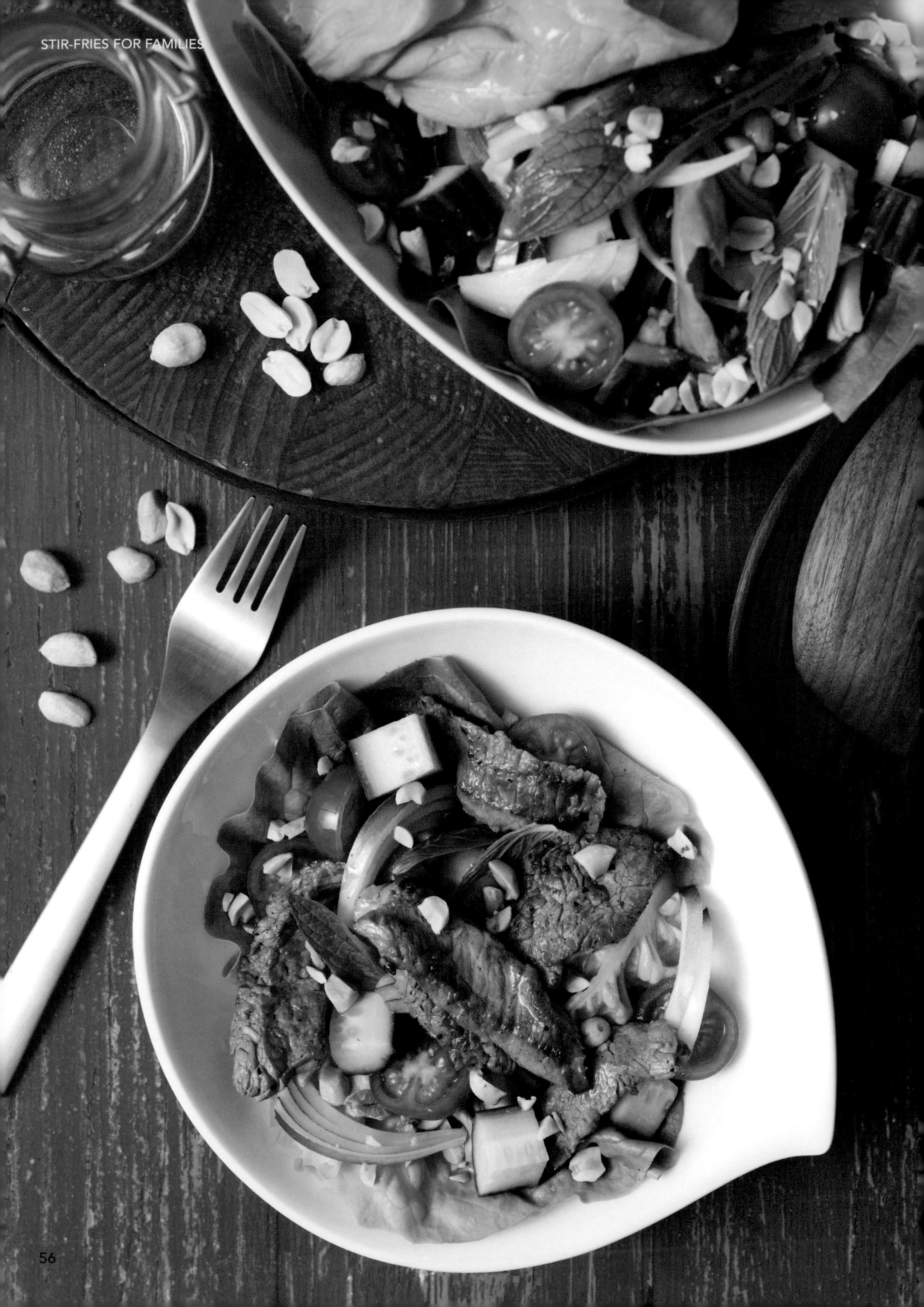

Beef mixture can be marinated for 30 minutes or overnight.

on the table in **25 MIN** serves **4**

VIETNAMESE BEEF SALAD

500g beef rump steak, sliced thinly
4 cloves garlic, crushed
2 teaspoons chinese cooking wine
2 teaspoons fish sauce
1 teaspoon caster sugar
1 medium butter lettuce, leaves separated
250g cherry tomatoes, halved
½ telegraph cucumber (200g), chopped coarsely
1 small red onion (100g), sliced thinly
1 cup loosely packed fresh mint leaves
1½ tablespoons rice vinegar
1 tablespoon olive oil
1 tablespoon peanut oil
¼ cup (35g) chopped roasted unsalted peanuts

1 Combine beef, garlic, cooking wine, sauce and sugar in medium bowl; cover, refrigerate.
2 Meanwhile, combine lettuce, tomato, cucumber, onion, mint, vinegar and olive oil in large bowl, season to taste.
3 Heat peanut oil in wok; stir-fry beef, in batches, until browned.
4 Divide salad among serving plates; top with beef, sprinkle with nuts.

nutritional count per serving 19.4 g total fat (4.1g saturated fat); 1371kJ (328 cal); 6.2g carbohydrate; 29.7g protein; 4.6g fibre

on the table in # 20 MIN serves 4

HONEYED GINGER CHICKEN

500g chicken thigh fillets, chopped coarsely
4cm piece fresh ginger (20g), grated
1 teaspoon five-spice powder
2 tablespoons peanut oil
170g asparagus, trimmed, cut into 3cm lengths
2 tablespoons dark soy sauce
2 tablespoons honey
1 tablespoon water
250g snow peas, trimmed, halved

1 Combine chicken, ginger, five-spice and half the oil in medium bowl.

2 Heat half the remaining oil in wok; stir-fry chicken, in batches, until browned. Remove from wok.

3 Heat remaining oil in wok; stir-fry asparagus until tender. Return chicken to wok with sauce, honey, the water and peas; stir-fry until hot, season to taste.

nutritional count per serving 15.5g total fat (3.5g saturated fat); 1292kJ (309 cal); 15.6g carbohydrate; 26.4g protein; 2.1g fibre

Chicken mixture can be marinated for 30 minutes or overnight.
Serve with steamed jasmine rice.

on the table in **25 MIN** serves **4**

CHINESE CHICKEN FRIED RICE

2 tablespoons peanut oil
2 eggs, beaten lightly
500g chicken thigh fillets, sliced thinly
2 medium carrots (240g), chopped finely
1 cup (120g) frozen peas
3 cloves garlic, crushed
6 green onions, sliced thinly
4 cups cooked white long-grain rice
1 tablespoon light soy sauce

1   Heat 1 teaspoon of the oil in wok. Pour egg into wok; cook omelette, tilting wok, until omelette is barely set. Remove omelette from wok; roll tightly then slice thinly.
2   Heat 2 teaspoons of the remaining oil in wok; stir-fry chicken, in batches, until browned. Remove from wok.

3   Heat remaining oil in wok; stir-fry carrot until tender. Add peas, garlic and half the onion; stir-fry until onion softens. Return chicken to wok with rice and sauce; stir-fry until hot, season to taste.
4   Serve fried rice topped with omelette and remaining onion.

nutritional count per serving 19.1g total fat (4.5g saturated fat); 2199kJ (526 cal); 52.4g carbohydrate; 33.4 protein; 5.1g fibre

You need to cook about 1⅓ cups white long-grain rice the day before making this recipe. Spread it evenly onto a tray and refrigerate overnight.

on the table in **35 MIN** serves **4**

FRIED TOFU WITH PORK MINCE AND WOMBOK

600g silken firm tofu
½ cup (75g) cornflour
1 tablespoon water
½ cup (125 ml) chicken stock
1 tablespoon chinese cooking wine
1 tablespoon tomato paste
1 teaspoon caster sugar
1 tablespoon japanese soy sauce
1 clove garlic, crushed
4cm piece fresh ginger (20g), grated
1½ tablespoons peanut oil
1 small wombok (700g), shredded coarsely
115g fresh shiitake mushrooms, sliced thinly
vegetable oil, for deep-frying
400g pork mince
3 green onions, sliced thinly
¼ cup loosely packed fresh coriander leaves

1 Cut tofu into 24 cubes; spread, in single layer, on absorbent-paper-lined tray. Cover tofu with more absorbent paper; stand 10 minutes.
2 Blend 2 teaspoons of the cornflour with the water in small jug; stir in stock, cooking wine, paste, sugar, sauce, garlic and ginger.
3 Heat a third of the peanut oil in wok; stir-fry wombok until wilted. Place in large bowl; cover to keep warm.
4 Heat half the remaining peanut oil in wok; stir-fry mushrooms until tender. Remove from wok.
5 Heat oil for deep-frying in wide deep saucepan.
6 Heat remaining peanut oil in wok; stir-fry mince until browned. Return mushrooms to wok with cornflour mixture; stir-fry until sauce boils and thickens slightly, season to taste. Place in bowl with wombok; cover to keep warm.
7 Toss tofu in remaining cornflour to coat; shake off excess. Deep-fry tofu, in batches, until browned lightly. Drain on absorbent paper; place in bowl with wombok.
8 Add remaining ingredients to bowl with wombok mixture; toss gently to combine.
nutritional count per serving 25.4g total fat (5.4g saturated fat); 2031kJ (486 cal); 23.9g carbohydrate; 37.2g protein; 5.4g fibre

on the table in **20 MIN** serves 4

EGG NOODLES WITH CHICKEN

500g chicken thigh fillets, sliced thinly
2 tablespoons tamari
2 tablespoons mirin
4cm piece fresh ginger (20g), grated
2 cloves garlic, crushed
440g thin egg noodles
2 tablespoons peanut oil
8 green onions, cut into 4cm lengths
500g baby pak choy, chopped coarsely

1 Combine chicken, tamari, mirin, ginger and garlic in medium bowl.
2 Place noodles in large heatproof bowl, cover with boiling water; separate with fork, drain.
3 Drain chicken, reserve marinade. Heat half the oil in wok; stir-fry chicken, in batches, until browned. Remove from wok.
4 Heat remaining oil in same cleaned wok; stir-fry onion until softened. Return chicken to wok with reserved marinade; bring to the boil. Add noodles and pak choy; stir-fry until pak choy wilts, season to taste.

nutritional count per serving 16.3g total fat (3.6g saturated fat); 1701kJ (407 cal); 30.4g carbohydrate; 30.9g protein; 4g fibre

Chicken mixture can be marinated for 30 minutes or overnight.

on the table in **25 MIN** serves 4

CHICKEN AND SPINACH NOODLES

500g chicken thigh fillets, sliced thinly
¼ cup (60ml) japanese soy sauce
4cm piece fresh ginger (20g), grated
2 cloves garlic, crushed
300g dried rice stick noodles
2 tablespoons peanut oil
200g green beans, trimmed, chopped coarsely
150g button mushrooms, sliced thinly
¼ cup (60ml) water
2 teaspoons shrimp paste
300g spinach, trimmed, chopped coarsely

1 Combine chicken, sauce, ginger and garlic in medium bowl.
2 Place noodles in large heatproof bowl, cover with boiling water; stand until tender, drain.
3 Heat half the oil in wok; stir-fry chicken, in batches, until browned. Remove from wok.
4 Heat remaining oil in wok; stir-fry beans and mushrooms until tender. Return chicken to wok with noodles, the water and paste; stir-fry until hot. Add spinach; stir-fry until spinach wilts, season to taste.

nutritional count per serving 16.1g total fat (3.5g saturated fat); 1450kJ (347 cal); 19.5g carbohydrate; 28.8g protein; 4g fibre

Chicken mixture can be marinated for 30 minutes or overnight.

Chinese black vinegar is a dark-coloured vinegar with a smoky, malt flavour that works well in stir-fries, braises and marinades. It is available from Asian grocery stores and some larger supermarkets.

on the table in **30 MIN** serves **4**

FRIED CHICKEN WITH RED CABBAGE

2 eggs
⅓ cup (50g) cornflour
vegetable oil, for deep-frying
500g chicken breast fillets, sliced thinly
1 tablespoon peanut oil
3 green onions, sliced thinly
2 cloves garlic, crushed
4 cups (300g) finely shredded red cabbage
1 large carrot (180g), cut into matchsticks
¼ cup (55g) caster sugar
¼ cup (60ml) chinese black vinegar
2 tablespoons light soy sauce

1 Whisk eggs with cornflour in small bowl until smooth; season to taste.
2 Heat vegetable oil in deep wide saucepan. Dip chicken in egg mixture; drain off excess. Deep-fry chicken, in batches, until browned lightly; drain on absorbent paper.
3 Heat peanut oil in wok; stir-fry onion and garlic until fragrant. Return chicken to wok with cabbage, carrot and remaining ingredients; stir-fry until hot, season to taste.
nutritional count per serving 19.3g total fat (3.6g saturated fat);1822 kJ (436 cal); 29.2g carbohydrate; 34.3g protein; 4.4g fibre

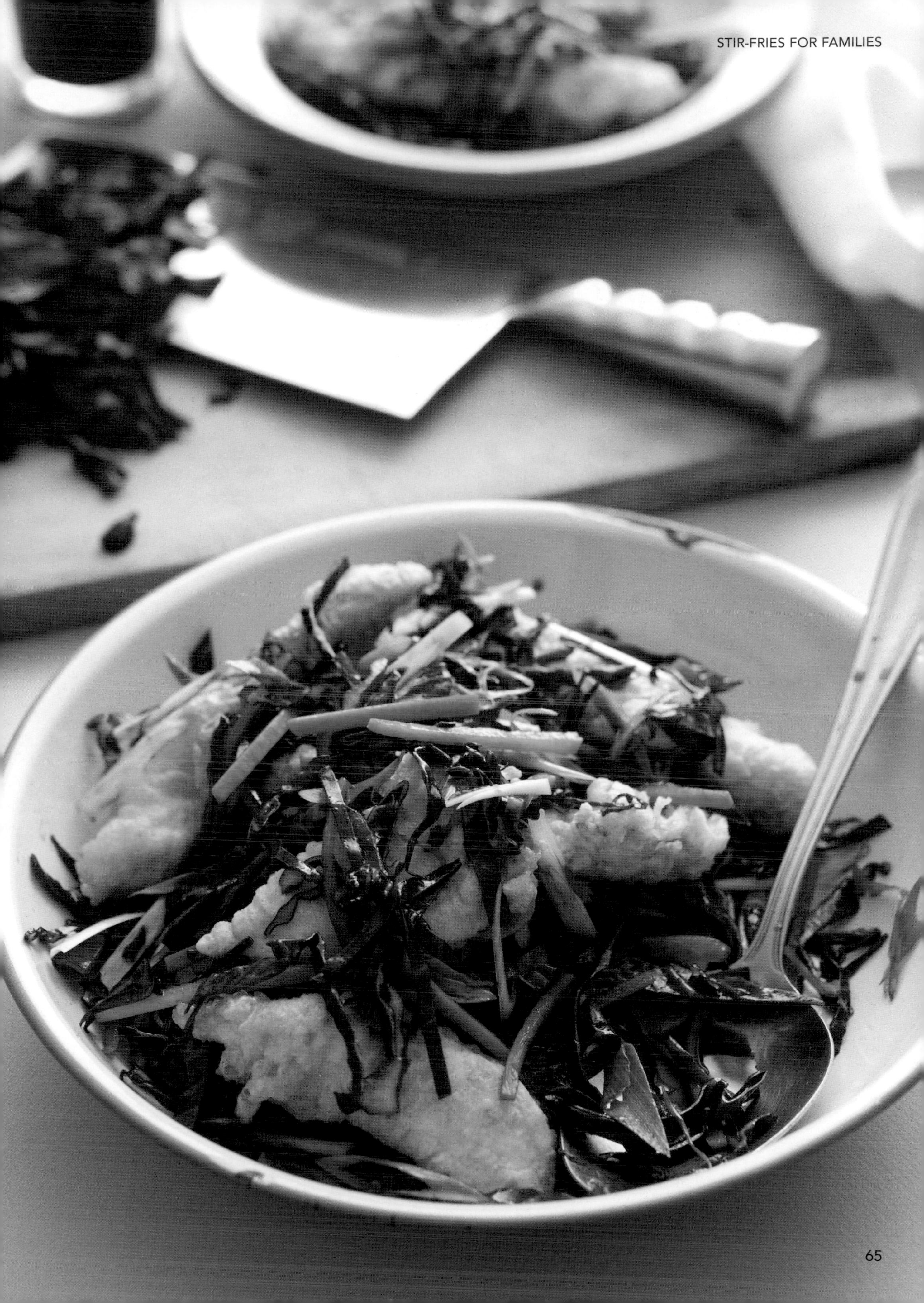

on the table in **35 MIN** serves **4**

SWEET AND SOUR DOUBLE-COOKED PORK

2 eggs
⅓ cup (50g) plain flour
1 tablespoon peanut oil
¼ cup (60ml) water
vegetable oil, for deep-frying
500g pork fillet, chopped coarsely
500g pineapple, peeled, cored, chopped coarsely
2 small red capsicums (300g), sliced thinly
¾ cup (185ml) chicken stock
¼ cup (60ml) white vinegar
2 tablespoons honey
1 tablespoon japanese soy sauce
1 tablespoon cornflour
2 tablespoons fresh coriander leaves

1   Whisk eggs, plain flour, 1 teaspoon of the peanut oil and half the water in medium bowl until smooth.
2   Heat vegetable oil in deep wide saucepan. Dip pork in egg mixture; drain off excess. Deep-fry pork, in batches, until browned lightly; drain on absorbent paper. Reheat oil; re-fry pork, in batches, until crisp. Drain on absorbent paper.
3   Heat remaining peanut oil in wok, stir-fry pineapple and capsicum until tender. Add stock, vinegar, honey and sauce; bring to the boil.
4   Blend cornflour with the remaining water in small bowl; add to wok. Stir-fry until sauce boils and thickens slightly. Return pork to wok; stir-fry until hot, season to taste. Sprinkle with coriander.
nutritional count per serving 31.4g total fat (5.4g saturated fat); 2307kJ (552 cal); 31.3g carbohydrate; 35g protein; 2.6g fibre

Serve with steamed jasmine rice.

66

on the table in # 20 MIN serves 4

FISH WITH KAFFIR LIME AND SUGAR SNAP PEAS

2 tablespoons peanut oil
500g firm white fish fillets, cut into 3cm pieces
1 medium brown onion (150g), sliced thinly
1 clove garlic, crushed
10cm stick fresh lemon grass (20g), chopped finely
1½ tablespoons brown sugar
½ cup (125ml) water
300g sugar snap peas, trimmed
170g asparagus, trimmed, cut into 3cm lengths
2 kaffir lime leaves, shredded finely
2 tablespoons lemon juice

1 Heat half the oil in wok; stir-fry fish, in batches, until browned. Remove from wok.
2 Heat remaining oil in wok; stir-fry onion, garlic and lemon grass until onion softens. Add sugar and half the water; bring to the boil. Simmer, uncovered, until sauce thickens slightly.
3 Add peas, asparagus and the remaining water; stir-fry until vegetables are tender. Return fish to wok; stir-fry until hot, season to taste.
4 Serve stir-fry sprinkled with lime leaves; drizzle with lemon juice.

nutritional count per serving 12.1g total fat (2.5g saturated fat); 1158kJ (277 cal); 11.2g carbohydrate; 29.5g protein; 3g fibre

We used blue-eye fillets in this recipe, but you can use any firm white fish fillets. Serve with steamed jasmine rice.

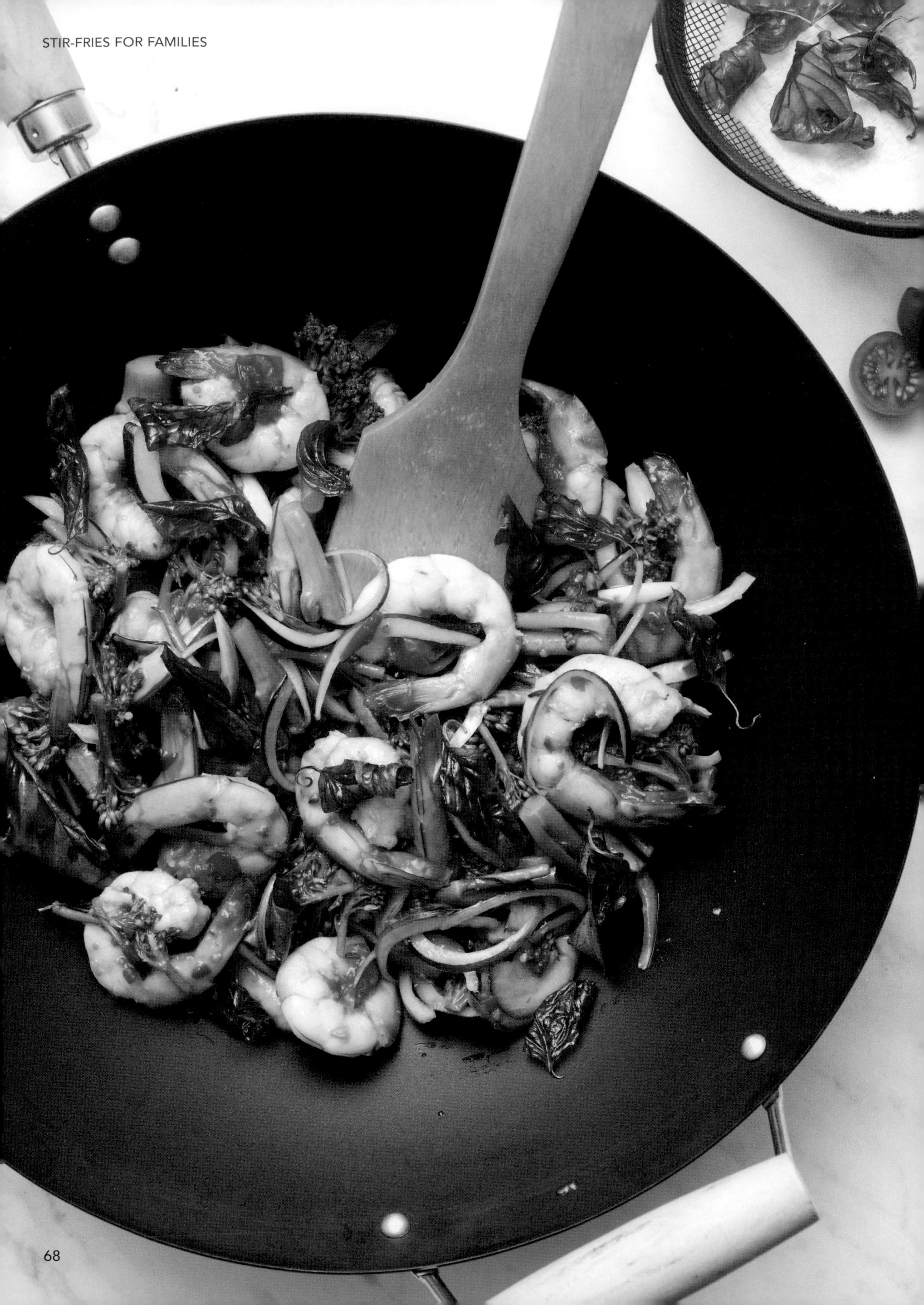

To save time purchase 500g shelled prawns for this recipe. Serve with steamed jasmine rice.

on the table in **35 MIN** serves **4**

PRAWNS WITH CRISPY THAI BASIL

1kg uncooked medium king prawns
vegetable oil, for shallow-frying
¼ cup loosely packed thai basil leaves
250g cherry tomatoes, halved
1 fresh long red chilli, chopped finely
¼ cup (60ml) sweet chilli sauce
2 tablespoons water
1 tablespoon brown sugar
350g broccolini, cut into 3cm lengths
1 medium red onion (170g), sliced thinly

1 Shell and devein prawns leaving tails intact.
2 Heat oil in wok; shallow-fry basil leaves, in batches, until crisp. Drain on absorbent paper. Remove oil from wok (cool and save for another use).
3 Add tomato, chilli, sauce, the water and sugar to same heated wok; stir-fry about 8 minutes or until mixture is thickened slightly. Add prawns, broccolini and onion to wok; stir-fry until prawns change colour, season to taste. Serve stir-fry topped with crisp basil leaves.

nutritional count per serving 6.3g total fat (0.8g saturated fat); 986kJ (236 cal); 10.5g carbohydrate; 31g protein; 6.1g fibre

on the table in # 30 MIN serves 4

THAI PORK MINCE

450g fresh wide rice noodles
1 tablespoon peanut oil
1 medium red onion (170g), sliced thinly
10cm stick fresh lemon grass (20g),
  chopped finely
5cm piece fresh ginger (25g), grated
2 cloves garlic, crushed
600g pork mince
2 tablespoons massaman curry paste
2 tablespoons lime juice
1 tablespoon fish sauce
1 tablespoon brown sugar
227g can water chestnut slices, rinsed,
  drained, chopped coarsely
½ cup firmly packed thai basil leaves

1 Place noodles in large heatproof bowl, cover with boiling water; separate with fork, drain.
2 Heat oil in wok; stir-fry onion, lemon grass, ginger and garlic until onion softens. Add mince; stir-fry until browned. Add curry paste; stir-fry until fragrant. Add juice, sauce and sugar; stir-fry 1 minute.
3 Add noodles to wok with water chestnuts and half the basil; stir-fry until hot, season to taste. Serve noodles sprinkled with remaining basil.
nutritional count per serving 19.5g total fat (5.1g saturated fat); 1910kJ (457 cal); 34g carbohydrate; 34.3g protein; 3.7g fibre

on the table in **35 MIN** serves **4**

STICKY PORK

600g pork neck, cut into 2cm pieces
2 tablespoons hoisin sauce
2 tablespoons dark soy sauce
1 tablespoon honey
1 tablespoon brown sugar
2 teaspoons dry sherry
1 teaspoon five-spice powder
3 cloves garlic, crushed
2 tablespoons peanut oil
350g gai lan, chopped coarsely
4 green onions, cut into 4cm lengths
1 lime, quartered

1 Combine pork, sauces, honey, sugar, sherry, five-spice and garlic in medium bowl.
2 Heat oil in wok; stir-fry pork, in batches, until browned all over. Return pork to wok; stir-fry until pork is cooked. Add gai lan, stir-fry until wilted. Remove from heat; stir in onion. Season to taste; serve with lime wedges.
nutritional count per serving 25.6g total fat (7.7g saturated fat); 1760kJ (421 cal); 14.7g carbohydrate; 31.1g protein; 4.8g fibre

Serve with steamed jasmine rice.

on the table in **30 MIN** serves **4**

ALMOND AND CHILLI CHICKEN

1 tablespoon peanut oil
½ cup (80g) blanched almonds
600g chicken breast fillets, sliced thinly
2 cloves garlic, crushed
2cm piece fresh ginger (10g), grated
2 teaspoons sambal oelek
1 tablespoon oyster sauce
1 tablespoon salt-reduced soy sauce
1 tablespoon dry sherry
6 green onions, cut into 3cm lengths

1 Heat 1 teaspoon of the oil in wok; stir-fry nuts until browned lightly. Remove from wok.
2 Heat remaining oil in wok; stir-fry chicken, in batches, until browned. Remove from wok.
3 Add garlic, ginger and sambal to wok; stir-fry until fragrant. Return nuts and chicken to wok with sauces and sherry; stir-fry until hot. Add onion; stir-fry until combined, season to taste.
nutritional count per serving 18.2g total fat (2.3g saturated fat); 1417kJ (339 cal); 3.1g carbohydrate; 38.2g protein; 2.3g fibre

Serve with steamed jasmine rice.

on the table in **35 MIN** serves **4**

FRIED BROWN RICE

1½ tablespoons peanut oil
3 eggs, beaten lightly
1 teaspoon sesame oil
115g baby corn, quartered
4 green onions, sliced thinly
2 cloves garlic, crushed
3 cups (500g) cooked brown long-grain rice
4 slices ham (100g), sliced thinly
2 tablespoons coarsely chopped
  fresh garlic chives
2 tablespoons salt-reduced soy sauce

1 Heat 1 teaspoon of the peanut oil in wok; pour half the egg into wok, tilting wok to make a thin omelette, cook until almost set. Remove omelette from wok; roll tightly then slice thinly. Repeat with another teaspoon of the peanut oil and remaining egg.
2 Heat remaining peanut oil and sesame oil in wok; stir-fry corn, onion and garlic until vegetables soften. Return omelette to wok with rice, ham, garlic chives and sauce; stir-fry until hot, season to taste.

nutritional count per serving 15.5g total fat (3.6g saturated fat); 1639kJ (392 cal); 45.2g carbohydrate; 15.8g protein; 3.5g fibre

You need to cook 1½ cups brown long-grain rice the night before making this recipe. Spread it evenly onto a tray and refrigerate overnight.

on the table in # 35 MIN serves 4

SINGAPORE NOODLES

400g cooked medium king prawns
250g dried thin egg noodles
1½ tablespoons peanut oil
4 eggs, beaten lightly
1 medium brown onion (150g), chopped finely
2 cloves garlic, crushed
1 tablespoon red curry paste
200g pork mince
200g chinese barbecued pork, sliced thinly
4 green onions, chopped coarsely
2 tablespoons salt-reduced soy sauce
1 tablespoon oyster sauce
1 fresh small red thai chilli, chopped finely

1 Shell and devein prawns; chop prawns coarsely.
2 Cook noodles in large saucepan of boiling water until tender; drain.
3 Heat 1 teaspoon of the oil in wok; pour half the egg into wok, tilting wok to make a thin omelette, cook until almost set. Remove omelette from wok; roll tightly then slice thinly. Repeat with another teaspoon of the oil and remaining egg.
4 Heat remaining oil in wok; stir-fry brown onion and garlic until onion softens. Add paste; stir-fry until fragrant. Add mince; stir-fry until browned. Add noodles, pork, prawns, half the green onion, sauces, chilli and half the omelette; stir-fry until hot. Season to taste; serve noodles topped with remaining omelette and onions.

nutritional count per serving 21.5g total fat (5.6g saturated fat); 2575kJ (616 cal); 48.5g carbohydrate; 54.7g protein; 3.1g fibre

To save time purchase 200g cooked shelled prawns for this recipe.

on the table in **30 MIN** serves **4**

HONEY SESAME BEEF STIR-FRY

450g thin hokkien noodles
1 tablespoon peanut oil
600g beef strips
115g baby corn, halved lengthways
4 green onions, cut into 4cm lengths
½ cup (70g) roasted unsalted peanuts
2 tablespoons honey
2 tablespoons salt-reduced soy sauce
1 tablespoon oyster sauce
2 tablespoons water
2 teaspoons sesame oil
1 tablespoon toasted sesame seeds

1 Place noodles in large heatproof bowl, cover with boiling water; separate with fork, drain.
2 Heat half the peanut oil in wok; stir-fry beef, in batches, until browned. Remove from wok.
3 Heat remaining peanut oil in wok; stir-fry corn and onion until corn is tender. Return beef to wok with noodles, nuts and combined honey, sauces, the water and sesame oil; stir-fry until hot, season to taste.
4 Serve noodles sprinkled with sesame seeds.
nutritional count per serving 22g total fat (4.1g saturated fat); 2596kJ (621 cal); 49.5g carbohydrate; 53.7g protein; 4.8g fibre

on the table in **25 MIN** serves **4**

HOISIN DUCK WITH ASIAN GREENS

1 chinese barbecued duck (1kg)
1 tablespoon peanut oil
2 cloves garlic, sliced thinly
3cm piece fresh ginger (15g), grated
1 fresh long red chilli, sliced thinly
350g gai lan, chopped coarsely
1 tablespoon water
1 tablespoon hoisin sauce
2 teaspoons salt-reduced soy sauce
4 green onions, cut into 3cm lengths

1 Quarter duck; discard bones. Slice duck meat thickly. Coarsely chop skin; measure ⅓ cup.
2 Heat 1 teaspoon of the oil in wok; stir-fry duck skin until crisp. Drain on absorbent paper.
3 Heat remaining oil in wok; stir-fry garlic, ginger and chilli until fragrant. Add gai lan, the water, sauces and half the onions; stir-fry until gai lan wilts. Add duck meat and skin, and remaining green onions; stir-fry until hot, season to taste.
nutritional count per serving 42.1g total fat (12g saturated fat); 2169kJ (519 cal); 3.6g carbohydrate; 30.7g protein; 4.3g fibre

Serve with steamed jasmine rice and lime wedges.

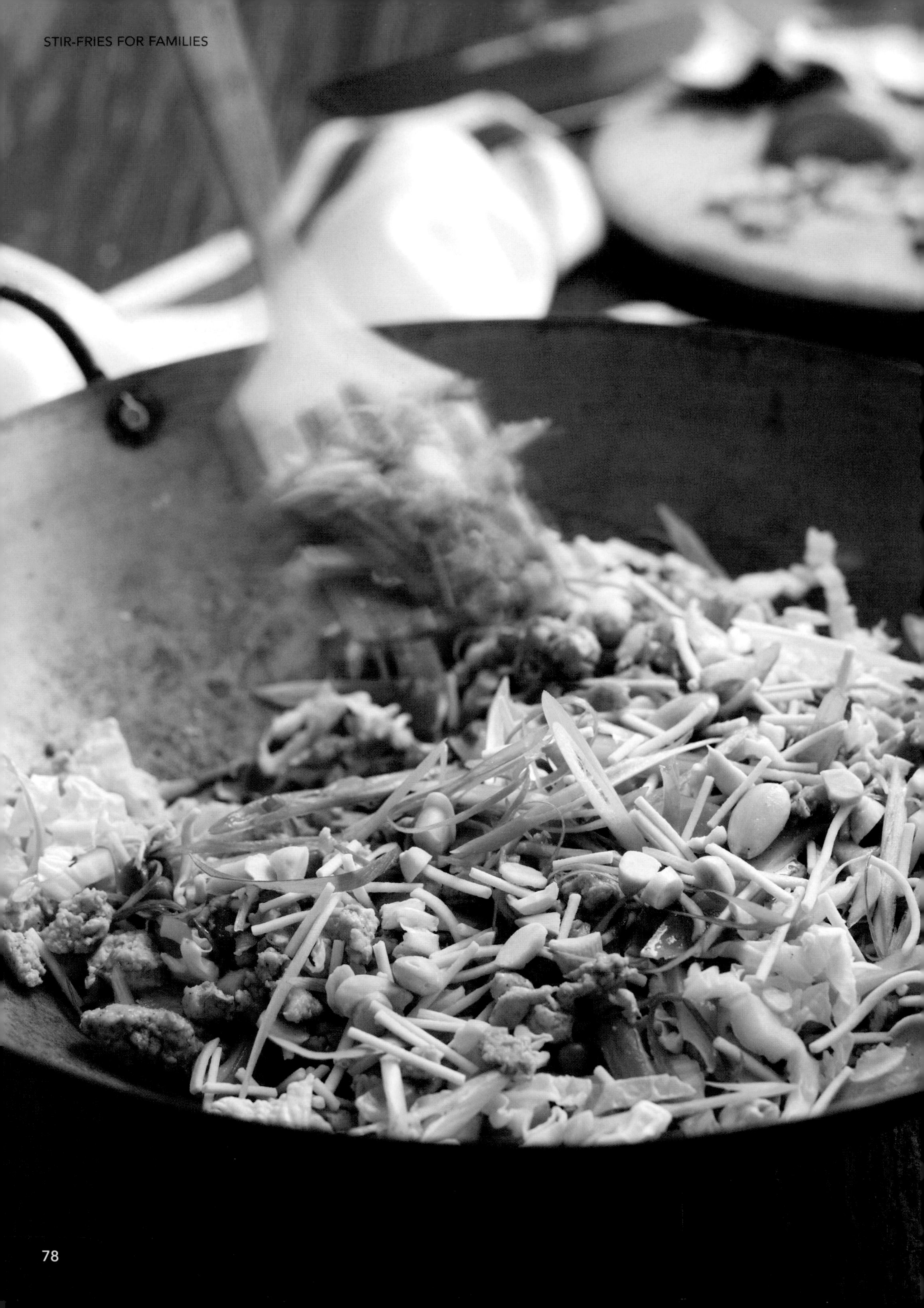

on the table in **25 MIN** serves **4**

CHOW MEIN

1 tablespoon peanut oil
500g turkey mince
1 medium red onion (170g), chopped finely
2 cloves garlic, crushed
1 tablespoon mild curry powder
2 stalks celery (300g), trimmed, chopped finely
1 medium carrot (120g), grated coarsely
¼ cup (60ml) salt-reduced chicken stock
2 tablespoons oyster sauce
1 tablespoon japanese soy sauce
2 cups (160g) finely shredded wombok
1 cup (120g) frozen baby peas
100g fried noodles
⅓ cup (55g) coarsely chopped roasted
   blanched almonds
2 green onions, sliced thinly

1 Heat oil in wok; stir-fry mince, red onion and garlic until mince changes colour. Add curry powder; stir-fry until fragrant. Add celery and carrot; stir-fry until vegetables are tender. Add stock, sauces, wombok and peas; stir-fry until wombok wilts.

2 Serve stir-fry sprinkled with noodles, nuts and green onions.

nutritional count per serving 26.1g total fat (5.8g saturated fat); 1860kJ (445 cal); 16.8g carbohydrate; 32.4g protein; 7.2g fibre

Chicken or pork mince can be used instead of turkey mince.

on the table in **25 MIN** serves **4**

LAMB WITH BROCCOLINI

1 tablespoon peanut oil
600g lamb strips
2 teaspoons sesame oil
1 medium red onion (170g), cut into thin wedges
2 cloves garlic, crushed
350g broccolini, cut into 3cm lengths
250g sugar snap peas, trimmed
1 tablespoon water
2 tablespoons sweet chilli sauce
1 tablespoon japanese soy sauce

1   Heat peanut oil in wok; stir-fry lamb, in batches, until browned. Remove from wok.
2   Heat sesame oil in wok; stir-fry onion and garlic until onion softens. Add broccolini, peas and the water; stir-fry until vegetables soften.
3   Return lamb to wok with sauces; stir-fry until hot, season to taste.

nutritional count per serving 14.6g total fat (3.6g saturated fat); 1404kJ (336 cal); 8g carbohydrate; 39.7g protein; 6.3g fibre

Serve with steamed jasmine rice.

on the table in 25 MIN serves 4

LEMON CHICKEN WITH ASIAN GREENS

2 tablespoons peanut oil
500g chicken thigh fillets, sliced thinly
10cm stick fresh lemon grass (20g),
  chopped finely
3 cloves garlic, crushed
600g gai lan, trimmed, cut into 5cm lengths
1 small yellow capsicum (150g), sliced thinly
2 tablespoons lemon juice
2 tablespoons light soy sauce

1 Heat half the oil in wok; stir-fry chicken, in batches, until browned. Remove from wok.
2 Heat remaining oil in wok; stir-fry lemon grass and garlic until fragrant. Add gai lan, capsicum, juice and sauce; stir-fry until vegetables are tender.
3 Return chicken to wok; stir-fry until hot, season to taste.

nutritional count per serving 15.6g total fat (3.5g saturated fat); 1162kJ (278 cal); 3.3g carbohydrate; 27.7g protein; 6.2g fibre

Serve with steamed jasmine rice.

on the table in **35 MIN** serves **4**

CHILLI BLACK BEAN MUSSELS

1kg mussels
1 cup (250ml) water
1 tablespoon peanut oil
1 small red capsicum (150g), sliced thinly
2 shallots (50g), sliced thinly
1 fresh long red chilli, sliced thinly
3 cloves garlic, sliced thinly
350g baby buk choy, chopped coarsely
2cm piece fresh ginger (10g), sliced thinly
¼ cup (60ml) chinese cooking wine
1 tablespoon black bean sauce
1 tablespoon oyster sauce
½ teaspoon sesame oil
2 teaspoons caster sugar
⅓ cup firmly packed fresh coriander leaves

1 Combine mussels and the water in wok; cook, covered, about 5 minutes or until mussels open (discard any that do not). Remove mussels from wok; reserve ½ cup cooking liquid.
2 Heat peanut oil in wok; stir-fry capsicum, shallot, chilli, garlic, buk choy and ginger until capsicum is tender. Add cooking wine; simmer, uncovered, until liquid reduces by half. Add reserved cooking liquid, sauces, sesame oil and sugar; stir-fry 1 minute. Return mussels to wok; stir-fry until hot. Sprinkle with coriander to serve.

nutritional count per serving 6.6g total fat (1.2g saturated fat); 614kJ (147 cal); 10.3g carbohydrate; 8.3g protein; 2.3g fibre

Serve with steamed jasmine rice.

on the table in # 35 MIN serves 4

PLUM CHICKEN WITH CASHEWS

2 tablespoons peanut oil
600g chicken breast fillets, sliced thinly
1 medium brown onion (150g), sliced thinly
2 cloves garlic, sliced thinly
1 medium red capsicum (200g), sliced thinly
1 medium yellow capsicum (200g), sliced thinly
1 medium carrot (120g), cut into matchsticks
115g baby corn, halved lengthways
⅓ cup (80ml) plum sauce
2 tablespoons japanese soy sauce
⅓ cup (50g) roasted unsalted cashews
⅓ cup firmly packed fresh coriander leaves

1 Heat half the oil in wok; stir-fry chicken, in batches, until browned. Remove from wok.
2 Heat remaining oil in wok; stir-fry onion and garlic until onion softens. Add capsicums, carrot, corn and sauces; stir-fry until vegetables are tender. Return chicken to wok with nuts and coriander; stir-fry until hot, season to taste.

nutritional count per serving 18.4g total fat (3.6g saturated fat); 1814kJ (434 cal); 25.4g carbohydrate; 39.6g protein; 4.6g fibre

Serve with steamed jasmine rice and lemon wedges.

on the table in ## 35 MIN serves 4

FIVE-SPICED CHICKEN AND NOODLES

250g dried thin egg noodles
600g chicken breast fillets, sliced thinly
2 tablespoons cornflour
1 teaspoon five-spice powder
2 tablespoons peanut oil
1 medium red capsicum (200g), sliced thinly
3 cloves garlic, crushed
3cm piece fresh ginger (15g), grated
1 cup (80g) bean sprouts
4 green onions, sliced thinly
2 tablespoons dark soy sauce
2 tablespoons sweet chilli sauce
2 tablespoons water

1 Cook noodles in large saucepan of boiling water until tender; drain.
2 Combine chicken, cornflour and five-spice in medium bowl. Heat half the oil in wok; stir-fry chicken, in batches, until browned. Remove from wok.
3 Heat remaining oil in wok; stir-fry capsicum, garlic and ginger until capsicum is tender. Return chicken to wok with noodles, sprouts, onion, sauces and the water; stir-fry until hot, season to taste.

nutritional count per serving 12.9g total fat (2.7g saturated fat); 2153kJ (515 cal); 53g carbohydrate; 43.6g protein; 3.6g fibre

To save time, purchase 500g shelled prawns for this recipe. Serve with steamed jasmine rice.

on the table in  **35 MIN** serves **4**

HONEYED PRAWNS

1kg uncooked medium king prawns
1 cup (150g) self-raising flour
1¼ cups (310ml) water
1 egg
⅓ cup (50g) cornflour
vegetable oil, for deep-frying
⅓ cup (120g) honey
1 tablespoon toasted sesame seeds
2 green onions, sliced thinly

1 Shell and devein prawns leaving tails intact.
2 Sift flour into medium bowl; gradually whisk in the water and egg until batter is smooth. Toss prawns in cornflour; shake off excess. Dip prawns in batter, one at a time, without coating the tails; shake off excess.
3 Heat vegetable oil in wok; deep-fry prawns, in batches, until browned lightly. Remove from wok; drain on absorbent paper.
4 Meanwhile, place honey in small saucepan; bring to the boil. Remove from heat.
5 Divide prawns between serving bowls; drizzle with honey, sprinkle with seeds and green onions.
nutritional count per serving 19.1g total fat (2.7g saturated fat); 2282kJ (546 cal); 61.6g carbohydrate; 31.9g protein; 1.8g fibre

on the table in 30 MIN serves 4

LEMON, CHILLI AND HERB SQUID

600g cleaned squid hoods
2 cloves garlic, crushed
1 tablespoon chermoula spice mix
1 teaspoon finely grated lemon rind
2 tablespoons olive oil
100g asian baby greens
½ cup firmly packed fresh mint leaves
½ cup firmly packed fresh coriander leaves
LEMON DRESSING
¼ cup (60ml) lemon juice
1 tablespoon olive oil
½ teaspoon caster sugar

1 Make lemon dressing.
2 Cut squid down centre to open out; score inside in diagonal pattern then cut into 3cm strips. Combine squid, garlic, spice mix, rind and half the oil in medium bowl.
3 Heat remaining oil in wok; stir-fry squid, in batches, until tender.
4 Divide asian greens, herbs and squid between serving plates; drizzle with lemon dressing.
lemon dressing Combine ingredients in screw-top jar; shake well, season to taste.
nutritional count per serving 15.6g total fat (2.5g saturated fat); 1058kJ (253 cal); 1.7g carbohydrate; 25.7g protein; 1g fibre

on the table in **35 MIN** serves **4**

THAI GREEN PORK

2 tablespoons peanut oil
600g pork fillet, sliced thinly
2 tablespoons green curry paste
2 baby eggplants (120g), chopped coarsely
1 large zucchini (150g), chopped coarsely
115g baby corn, halved lengthways
270ml can coconut milk
2 fresh kaffir lime leaves, shredded finely
1 tablespoon lime juice
1 tablespoon fish sauce
2 teaspoons brown sugar
⅓ cup coarsely chopped fresh coriander leaves

1 Heat half the oil in wok; stir-fry pork, in batches, until browned. Remove from wok.
2 Heat remaining oil in wok; stir-fry curry paste until fragrant. Add eggplant, zucchini and corn; stir-fry until vegetables are tender. Add coconut milk, kaffir lime leaves, juice, sauce and sugar; stir-fry 2 minutes. Return pork to wok; stir-fry until hot, season to taste. Serve stir-fry sprinkled with coriander.

nutritional count per serving 28.9g total fat (14.9g saturated fat); 1940kJ (464 cal); 11.4g carbohydrate; 37.7g protein; 5g fibre

Serve with steamed jasmine rice.

89

Serve nasi goreng with sliced cucumber and tomato.
To save time purchase 300g shelled prawns for this recipe.

on the table in **35 MIN** serves **4**

NASI GORENG COMBO

600g uncooked medium king prawns
1 teaspoon sesame oil
1 tablespoon peanut oil
1 medium brown onion (150g), chopped finely
3 cloves garlic, crushed
5cm piece fresh ginger (25g), grated
1 tablespoon sambal oelek
2 chicken thigh fillets (200g), cut into 2cm pieces
3 cups (450g) cooked white long-grain rice
2 cups (160g) finely shredded wombok
1 cup (80g) bean sprouts
4 green onions, sliced thinly
1 tablespoon kecap manis
4 eggs

1 Shell and devein prawns; chop prawns coarsely.
2 Heat sesame oil with half the peanut oil in wok; stir-fry onion, garlic, ginger and sambal until onion softens. Add chicken; stir-fry until browned. Add prawns; stir-fry until prawns change colour. Add rice, wombok, sprouts, onion and kecap manis; stir-fry until hot, season to taste.
3 Meanwhile, heat remaining peanut oil in large frying pan; fry eggs, one side only, until barely set.
4 Serve bowls of nasi goreng topped with eggs.
nutritional count per serving 15.2g total fat (3.7g saturated fat); 1822kJ (436 cal); 36.1g carbohydrate; 36.9g protein; 2.8g fibre

You need to cook 1½ cups (300g) white long-grain rice the night before making this recipe. Spread it evenly onto a tray and refrigerate overnight.

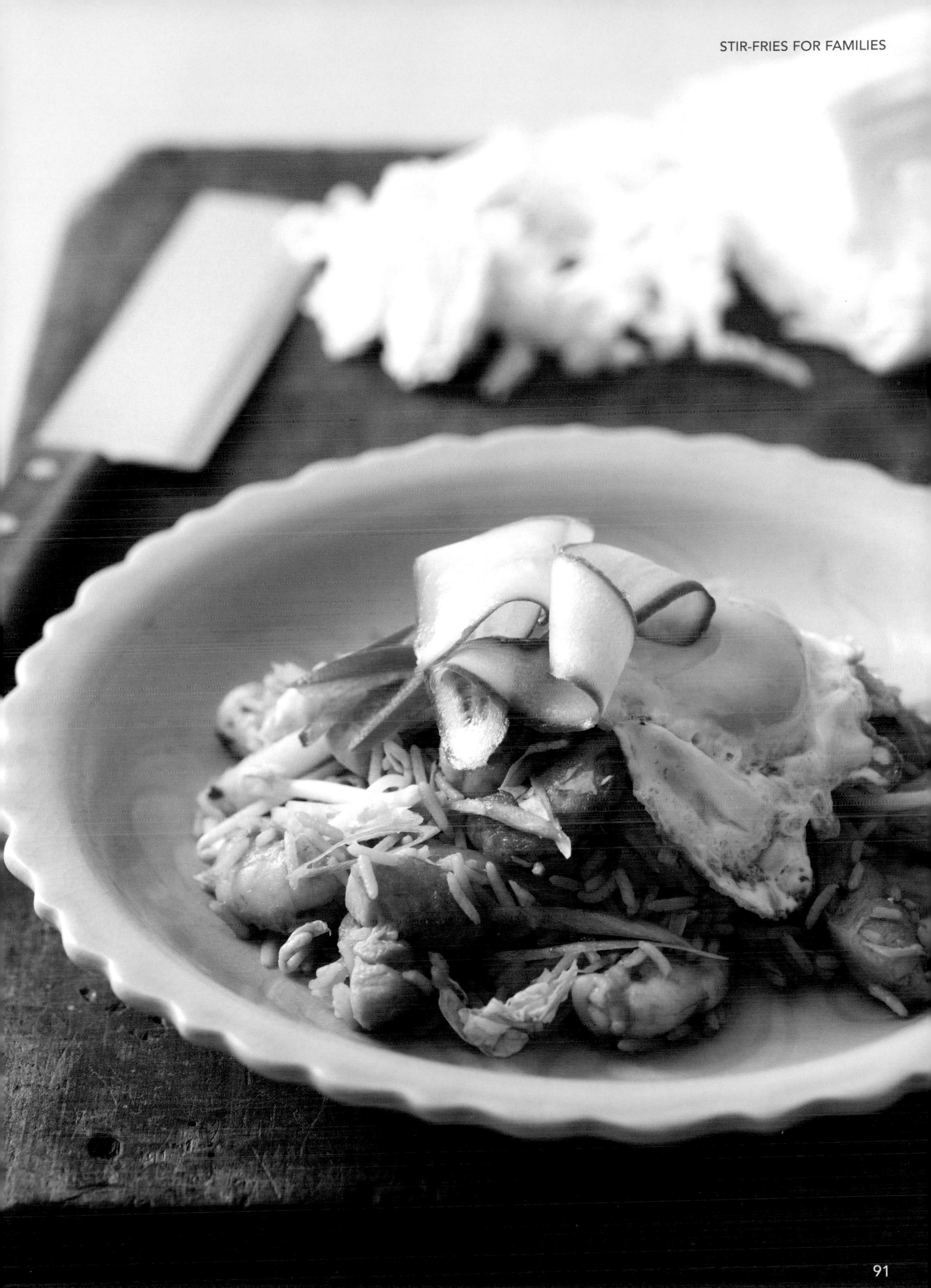

on the table in **25 MIN** serves **4**

HOISIN LAMB

1 tablespoon peanut oil
1 large brown onion (200g), chopped finely
2 cloves garlic, crushed
5cm piece fresh ginger (25g), grated
1 fresh long red chilli, chopped finely
600g lamb mince
¼ cup (60ml) hoisin sauce
2 tablespoons lime juice
227g can water chestnut slices, rinsed,
  drained, chopped finely
250g (3 cups) bean sprouts
1 cup loosely packed fresh mint leaves
8 large iceberg lettuce leaves

1   Heat oil in wok; stir-fry onion, garlic, ginger and chilli until onion softens. Add mince; stir-fry until browned. Add sauce, juice, chestnuts, sprouts and half the mint; stir-fry until hot, season to taste.
2   Divide lamb mixture between lettuce leaves; sprinkle with remaining mint.
nutritional count per serving 17.2g total fat (6.1g saturated fat); 1505kJ (360 cal); 13.8g carbohydrate; 34.5g protein; 6.6g fibre

on the table in **30 MIN** serves **4**

CHILLI AND BASIL SQUID

600g squid hoods, cut into 1cm rings
1 fresh long red chilli, chopped finely
2 cloves garlic, crushed
⅓ cup coarsely chopped fresh basil leaves
1 tablespoon olive oil
1 medium red onion (170g), sliced thinly
1 chorizo sausage (170g), sliced thinly
250g cherry tomatoes, halved
⅓ cup (85g) bottled tomato pasta sauce
⅓ cup loosely packed fresh baby basil leaves
1 medium lemon (140g), cut into wedges

1 Combine squid, chilli, garlic, chopped basil and oil in medium bowl.
2 Heat wok; stir-fry squid mixture, in batches, until tender. Remove from wok. Stir-fry onion and chorizo in wok until onion softens and chorizo is browned. Return squid to wok with tomato, sauce and half the basil leaves; stir-fry until hot.
3 Serve stir-fry topped with remaining basil leaves; accompany with lemon wedges.

nutritional count per serving 19.5g total fat (5.9g saturated fat); 1471kJ (352 cal); 7.6g carbohydrate; 34.9g protein; 3.2g fibre

Serve with a green salad.

93

CRISPY BEEF SANG CHOY BOW

on the table in 20 min serves 4

Heat oiled wok; stir-fry 2 thinly sliced green onions until soft. Add 400g beef mince; stir-fry until browned. Add 1 cup frozen peas and ¼ cup hoisin sauce; stir-fry until hot. Remove from heat; stir in 100g crispy fried noodles and another 2 thinly sliced green onions. Divide beef mixture between 8 large iceberg lettuce leaves.
nutritional count per serving
13.3g total fat (4.9g saturated fat); 1158kJ (277 cal); 13.8g carbohydrate; 23.7g protein; 4.5g fibre

For crisp lettuce cups stand lettuce leaves in a large bowl of iced water; drain then dry in salad spinner just before serving.

GINGER AND TERIYAKI CHICKEN

on the table in 20 min serves 4

Cut 2 medium carrots and 1 large red capsicum into matchsticks. Combine 500g thinly sliced chicken breast fillets and 4cm piece grated fresh ginger. Heat oiled wok; stir-fry chicken, in batches, until browned. Remove chicken from wok. Reheat wok; stir-fry carrot and capsicum until tender. Return chicken to wok with 2 tablespoons teriyaki sauce; stir-fry until hot, season to taste. Serve sprinkled with ¼ cup loosely packed fresh coriander leaves.
nutritional count per serving
4.6g total fat (1.1g saturated fat); 832kJ (199 cal); 8.1g carbohydrate; 29.8g protein; 2.2g fibre

Serve with steamed jasmine rice.

CURRIED FRIED RICE WITH VEGETABLES

on the table in 15 min serves 4

Heat oiled wok; pour in 2 lightly beaten eggs, tilting wok, until eggs are almost set. Remove omelette from wok; roll tightly then slice thinly. Heat 2 tablespoons vegetable oil in wok. Add 2 cups frozen combined peas and corn, 150g coarsely chopped ham and 1 tablespoon curry powder; stir-fry until fragrant. Add 4 cups cooked white long-grain rice; stir-fry until hot. Stir in omelette, season to taste.
nutritional count per serving
18.4g total fat (3.5g saturated fat); 1952kJ (467 cal); 55.6g carbohydrate; 17.4g protein; 4.4g fibre

STIR-FRIED CHICKEN AND EGG NOODLES

on the table in 20 min serves 4

Place 440g thin egg noodles in large heatproof bowl, cover with boiling water; separate with fork, drain. Heat 2 teaspoons vegetable oil in wok; stir-fry 500g thinly sliced chicken thigh fillets, in batches, until browned, remove from wok. Heat another 2 teaspoons vegetable oil in wok; stir-fry 115g halved baby corn, 120g packet cantonese sauce and ¼ cup water until corn is tender. Return chicken to wok with noodles; stir-fry until hot. Season to taste; serve stir-fry sprinkled with 2 thinly sliced green onions.

nutritional count per serving
12.1g total fat (2.6g saturated fat); 1818kJ (435 cal); 49.9g carbohydrate; 30g protein; 3.5g fibre

SWEET CHICKEN WITH CAPSICUM

on the table in 25 min serves 4

Cut 1 medium brown onion into wedges. Coarsely chop 1 medium red and 1 medium yellow capsicum. Heat 2 teaspoons vegetable oil in wok; stir-fry 500g coarsely chopped chicken thigh fillets, in batches, until browned. Remove chicken from wok. Heat another 2 teaspoons vegetable oil in wok; stir-fry onion, capsicum and 250g trimmed green beans until vegetables are tender. Return chicken to wok with ½ cup plum sauce and ¼ cup water; stir-fry until hot, season to taste.

nutritional count per serving
11.5g total fat (2.5g saturated fat); 1384kJ (331 cal); 29.7g carbohydrate; 26.2g protein; 3.4g fibre

LAMB WITH SPINACH AND RICE NOODLES

on the table in 20 min serves 4

Trim and coarsely shred 300g spinach. Place 300g dried rice stick noodles in large heatproof bowl, cover with boiling water; stand until tender, drain. Heat oiled wok; stir-fry 500g thinly sliced lamb fillet, in batches, until browned, remove lamb from wok. Reheat wok; stir-fry spinach and 2 crushed garlic cloves until spinach wilts. Return lamb to wok with noodles, ¼ cup kecap manis and 1 tablespoon japanese soy sauce; stir-fry until hot, season to taste.

nutritional count per serving
12.5g total fat (3.9g saturated fat); 1396kJ (334 cal); 15.2g carbohydrate; 38.4g protein; 1.7g fibre

TOFU PAD THAI

on the table in 15 min **serves** 4

Place 250g dried rice stick noodles in large heatproof bowl, cover with boiling water; stand until tender, drain. Meanwhile, cut 320g hard tofu into 2cm pieces. Cut 4 green onions into 4cm lengths. Heat oiled wok; stir-fry tofu, in batches, until browned. Remove from wok. Reheat wok; stir-fry onion and 2 teaspoons grated fresh ginger until onion softens. Return tofu to wok with noodles, 2 tablespoons pad thai sauce and 2 tablespoons lime juice; stir-fry until hot. Sprinkle with fresh coriander leaves to serve, if you like.
nutritional count per serving
8.9g total fat (1.3g saturated fat); 849kJ (203 cal); 16.2g carbohydrate; 10.9g protein; 7.1g fibre

CHAR SIU VEGETABLES

on the table in 15 min **serves** 4

Heat 1 tablespoon peanut oil in wok; stir-fry 1 thinly sliced medium red onion until soft. Add 350g coarsely chopped gai lan, 300g coarsely chopped choy sum and ¼ cup char siu sauce; stir-fry until greens wilt. Sprinkle with 1 tablespoon toasted sesame seeds before serving.
nutritional count per serving
7.3g total fat (1.1g saturated fat); 568kJ (136 cal); 10.3g carbohydrate; 4.4g protein; 6.8g fibre

Serve with steamed jasmine rice.

SWEET AND SOUR VEGETABLES

on the table in 15 min **serves** 4

Heat 1 tablespoon peanut oil in wok; stir-fry 800g packaged traditional stir-fry vegetables and 115g coarsely chopped baby corn until vegetables are tender. Add 225g can drained pineapple pieces, ½ cup sweet and sour sauce and 50g enoki mushrooms; stir-fry until hot, season to taste.
nutritional count per serving
5.4g total fat (0.9g saturated fat); 890kJ (213 cal); 31.8g carbohydrate; 5.2g protein; 8.8g fibre

SPICED PUMPKIN AND CHICKPEAS

on the table in 15 min **serves** 4

Cut 500g pumpkin into 1cm pieces.
Heat 2 tablespoons peanut oil
in wok; stir-fry pumpkin about
6 minutes or until almost tender.
Add 1 tablespoon chermoula
spice mix; stir-fry about 2 minutes
or until pumpkin is tender. Add
rinsed and drained 420g can
chickpeas and 350g coarsely
chopped spinach; stir-fry until
spinach wilts, season to taste.
nutritional count per serving
11g total fat (2.1g saturated fat),
828kJ (198 cal); 15.5g carbohydrate;
7.2g protein; 5.4g fibre

**Serve with steamed jasmine rice
and lemon wedges.**

VEGETABLES WITH CHILLI

on the table in 15 min **serves** 4

Heat oiled wok; stir-fry 400g packet
traditional stir-fry vegetables until
tender. Add 600g quartered baby
pak choy and ⅓ cup oriental soy,
garlic and honey sauce; stir-fry until
pak choy wilts. Add ½ cup roasted
unsalted cashews and ½ cup firmly
packed fresh mint leaves; stir-fry
until hot, season to taste. Serve
topped with 1 thinly sliced fresh
long red chilli.
nutritional count per serving
11.8g total fat (2g saturated fat);
790kJ (189 cal); 9.6g carbohydrate;
7.9g protein; 6.9g fibre

HALOUMI AND TOMATO

on the table in 15 min **serves** 4

Cut 250g haloumi cheese into
2cm pieces. Heat oiled wok;
stir-fry cheese, in batches, until
browned. Remove from wok.
Reheat wok; stir fry 4 thickly
sliced medium zucchini, 1 thickly
sliced medium red capsicum and
250g halved cherry tomatoes until
vegetables are tender. Return
cheese to wok with ⅓ cup bottled
tomato pasta sauce; stir-fry until
hot, season to taste. Serve
sprinkled with finely sliced fresh
basil leaves.
nutritional count per serving
13.6g total fat (7.3g saturated fat);
941kJ (225 cal); 8.1g carbohydrate;
16.1g protein; 3.9g fibre

STIR-FRIES FOR FRIENDS

on the table in **30 MIN** serves **4**

HONEY CHICKEN WITH BUK CHOY AND SESAME

600g chicken thigh fillets, chopped coarsely
¼ cup (60ml) light soy sauce
¼ cup (90g) honey
2cm piece fresh ginger (10g), grated
1 clove garlic, crushed
2 tablespoons finely chopped fresh coriander
1 tablespoon finely chopped vietnamese mint
1 tablespoon peanut oil
2 teaspoons sesame oil
1 small red onion (100g), sliced thinly
1 small red capsicum (150g), chopped coarsely
300g buk choy, trimmed, shredded finely
1 tablespoon black sesame seeds

1 Combine chicken, sauce, honey, ginger, garlic and herbs in medium bowl. Drain chicken; reserve marinade.
2 Heat peanut oil in wok; stir-fry chicken, in batches, until browned. Remove from wok.
3 Heat sesame oil in wok; stir-fry onion and capsicum until vegetables are tender. Add buk choy and reserved marinade; stir-fry until mixture boils and buk choy wilts. Return chicken to wok; stir-fry until hot, season to taste. Serve sprinkled with black sesame seeds.

nutritional count per serving 16.2g total fat (3.6g saturated fat); 1501kJ (359 cal); 22.4g carbohydrate; 30.7g protein; 2.1g fibre

Serve with steamed jasmine rice.
Chicken mixture can be marinated for
a few hours or overnight in the fridge.

Fresh salmon or ocean trout can be used in place of the tuna.

on the table in **30 MIN** serves **4**

FRIED NOODLES WITH CABBAGE AND TUNA

600g piece tuna, chopped coarsely
¼ cup (60ml) light soy sauce
1 tablespoon wasabi
1 tablespoon lime juice
1 tablespoon grated palm sugar
440g fresh thin egg noodles
2 tablespoons peanut oil
1½ cups (120g) finely shredded savoy cabbage
½ cup (125ml) sweet chilli sauce
1 tablespoon fish sauce
2 green onions, sliced thinly

1 Combine tuna, soy sauce, wasabi, juice and sugar in medium bowl. Drain tuna; reserve 2 tablespoons marinade.

2 Place noodles in large heatproof bowl, cover with boiling water; separate with fork, drain.

3 Heat half the oil in wok; stir-fry tuna, in batches, until cooked as desired. Remove from wok, season to taste.

4 Heat remaining oil in wok; stir-fry cabbage until wilted. Add noodles, reserved marinade, sweet chilli sauce and fish sauce; stir-fry until mixture boils, season to taste. Serve noodles topped with tuna and onions.

nutritional count per serving 19.7g total fat (5.7g saturated fat); 2220kJ (531 cal); 39.7g carbohydrate; 45.7g protein; 4.7g fibre

on the table in **30 MIN** serves **4**

PONZU PRAWNS WITH GREEN ONIONS AND SPINACH

1kg uncooked medium king prawns
⅓ cup (80ml) japanese soy sauce
2 tablespoons fish sauce
¼ cup (60ml) lime juice
2 tablespoons mirin
2 tablespoons grated palm sugar
2 tablespoons peanut oil
250g silver beet, trimmed, shredded finely
1 small yellow capsicum (150g), sliced thinly
2 sheets nori, shredded finely
1 lime, cut into wedges

1 Shell and devein prawns leaving heads and tails intact.
2 Combine prawns, sauces, juice, mirin and sugar in large bowl. Drain prawns; reserve ¼ cup marinade.
3 Heat half the oil in wok; stir-fry prawns, in batches, until changed in colour. Remove from wok.
4 Heat remaining oil in wok; stir-fry silver beet and capsicum until vegetables are tender. Return prawns to wok with reserved marinade and half the nori; stir-fry until mixture boils, season to taste. Serve sprinkled with remaining nori; accompany with lime.
nutritional count per serving 10.1g total fat (1.8g saturated fat); 1062kJ (254 cal); 9.5g carbohydrate; 28.9g protein; 1.4g fibre

Use sharp scissors to finely shred the nori. Prawn mixture can be marinated for a few hours or overnight in the fridge.

on the table in # 30 MIN serves 4

CASHEW CHICKEN WITH WATER CHESTNUTS AND BROCCOLI

600g chicken thigh fillets, chopped coarsely
2 tablespoons XO sauce
1 teaspoon fish sauce
2 tablespoons finely grated lemon rind
2 tablespoons lemon juice
1 tablespoon brown sugar
10cm stick fresh lemon grass (20g),
  chopped finely
2 tablespoons peanut oil
1 small brown onion (80g), sliced thinly
1 fresh long red chilli, sliced thinly
300g broccoli, cut into florets
227g can whole water chestnuts, rinsed, drained
2 green onions, sliced thinly
¼ cup (40g) coarsely chopped roasted unsalted
  cashew nuts

1 Combine chicken, sauces, rind, juice, sugar and lemon grass in medium bowl.
2 Heat half the oil in wok; stir-fry chicken, in batches, until browned. Remove from wok.
3 Heat remaining oil in wok; stir-fry brown onion and chilli until onion softens. Add broccoli and chestnuts; stir-fry until broccoli is tender. Return chicken to wok; stir-fry until hot, season to taste. Serve sprinkled with green onion and nuts.
nutritional count per serving 22.2g total fat (4.8g saturated fat); 1634kJ (391 cal); 10.8g carbohydrate; 34.4g protein; 5.4g fibre

Serve with steamed jasmine rice. XO sauce is a spicy seafood sauce made from dried fish and shrimp and cooked with chilli, onion, garlic and oil. It is available from Asian food stores.
Chicken mixture can be marinated for a few hours or overnight in the fridge.

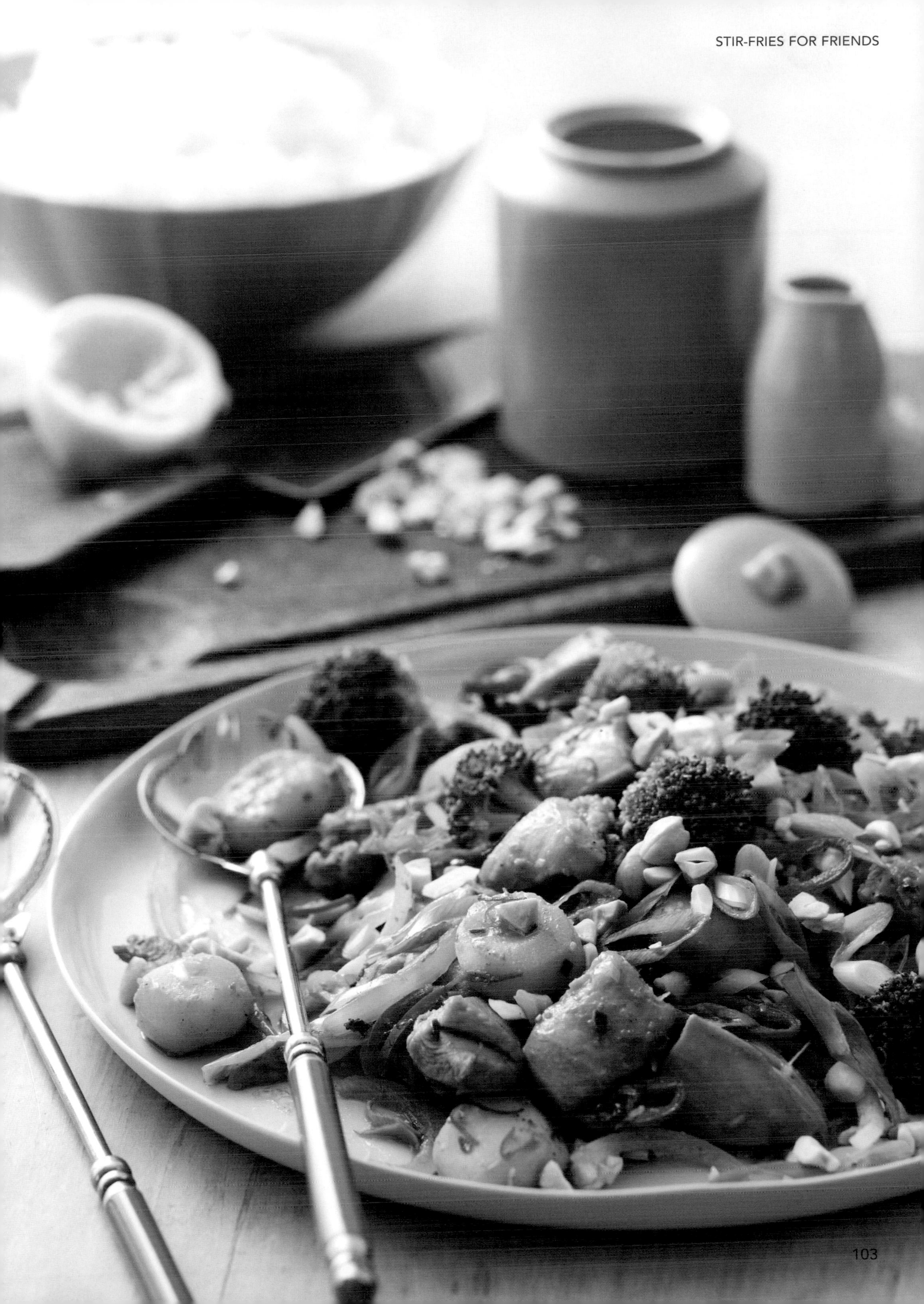

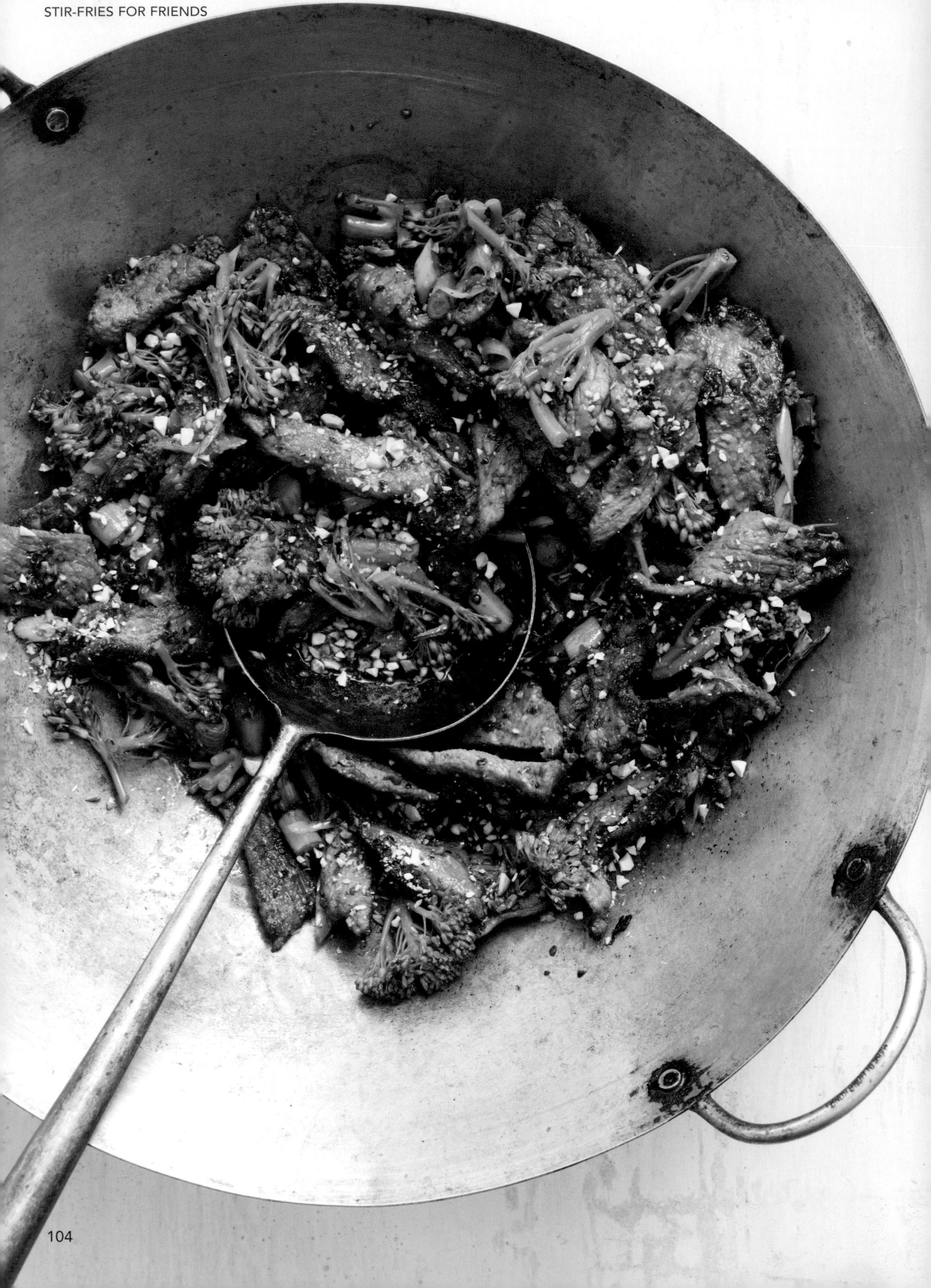

on the table in # 30 MIN serves 4

NUTTY BEEF WITH BROCCOLINI

600g beef scotch fillet steak, sliced thinly
2 tablespoons dukkah
½ cup (65g) finely chopped roasted
  unsalted pistachios
2 tablespoons peanut oil
2 teaspoons sesame oil
2 shallots (50g), sliced thinly
350g broccolini, trimmed, chopped coarsely
2 tablespoons kecap manis
2 tablespoons chinese cooking wine

1 Combine beef, dukkah and half the nuts in medium bowl.
2 Heat half the peanut oil in wok; stir-fry beef, in batches, until browned. Remove from wok.
3 Heat remaining peanut oil and sesame oil in wok; stir-fry shallots and broccolini until broccolini is tender. Return beef to wok with kecap manis and cooking wine; stir-fry until hot, season to taste. Serve sprinkled with remaining nuts.

nutritional count per serving 31.5g total fat (6.7g saturated fat); 2052kJ (491 cal); 4.2g carbohydrate; 43.8g protein; 5.3g fibre

After stir-frying beef, wipe out the wok with absorbent paper to prevent any remaining spices or nuts from burning and spoiling the stir-fry. The beef mixture can be marinated for a few hours or overnight in the fridge.

Dukkah is an Egyptian spice blend made of roasted nuts and aromatic spices. It is available from Middle-Eastern food stores, specialty spice stores and some supermarkets.

on the table in **30 MIN** serves **4**

SPICED LAMB WITH GREEN BEANS

600g lamb backstrap, sliced thinly
2 teaspoons ground allspice
¼ cup (55g) firmly packed brown sugar
¼ cup (60ml) worcestershire sauce
2 tablespoons peanut oil
300g green beans, trimmed
250g swiss brown mushrooms, quartered

1 Combine lamb, allspice, sugar and sauce in medium bowl. Drain lamb; reserve marinade.
2 Heat half the oil in wok; stir-fry lamb, in batches, until browned. Remove from wok.
3 Heat remaining oil in wok; stir-fry beans, mushrooms and reserved marinade until mixture boils and vegetables are tender. Return lamb to wok; stir-fry until hot, season to taste.
nutritional count per serving 17.9g total fat (4.8g saturated fat); 1613kJ (386 cal); 19.3g carbohydrate; 36g protein; 3.7g fibre

Serve with steamed rice.
Lamb mixture can be marinated for a few hours or overnight in the fridge.

on the table in **25 MIN** serves **4**

PORK IN RED CURRY PASTE

600g pork fillet, sliced thinly
¼ cup (75g) red curry paste
1 tablespoon hoisin sauce
2 teaspoons fish sauce
2 tablespoons peanut oil
150g fresh shiitake mushrooms, sliced thinly
200g baby carrots, trimmed
2 long green chillies, sliced thinly

1 Combine pork, paste and sauces in medium bowl.
2 Heat half the oil in wok; stir-fry pork, in batches, until browned. Remove from wok.
3 Heat remaining oil in wok; stir-fry mushrooms and carrots until tender. Return pork to wok; stir-fry until hot, season to taste.
4 Serve stir-fry sprinkled with chilli.
nutritional count per serving 18.9g total fat (3.5g saturated fat); 1467kJ (351 cal); 6.8g carbohydrate; 36.1g protein; 5.1g fibre

Serve with steamed jasmine rice. Pork mixture can be marinated for a few hours or overnight in the fridge.

on the table in **35 MIN** serves **4**

TEMPURA FISH WITH SOMEN NOODLES

270g dried somen noodles
²/₃ cup (90g) packaged tempura mix
½ cup (125ml) iced water
2 tablespoons lime juice
2 sheets nori
4 x 160g firm white fish fillets
vegetable oil, for deep-frying
2 teaspoons sesame oil
1 cup (50g) snow pea sprouts
½ cup fresh basil leaves, shredded finely
½ cup fresh mint leaves, shredded finely
SWEET AND SOUR SAUCE
½ cup (125ml) sweet chilli sauce
2 tablespoons japanese soy sauce
1 tablespoon fish sauce
2 tablespoons lime juice

1   Make sweet and sour sauce.
2   Cook noodles in large saucepan of boiling water until tender; drain.
3   Meanwhile, combine tempura mix, the water and juice in medium bowl; stir until batter is barely combined (mixture should be lumpy).
4   Cut nori into strips the same width as the fish; brush nori with a little water. Wrap nori tightly around fish.
5   Heat vegetable oil in wok. Dip fish parcels into batter; deep-fry, in two batches, until browned lightly and crisp. Drain on absorbent paper then slice thickly.
6   Heat sesame oil in wok; stir-fry noodles, sprouts, herbs and half the sweet and sour sauce until hot, season to taste.
7   Serve noodles topped with fish; drizzle with remaining sauce. Accompany with lime wedges.
sweet and sour sauce Bring sauces to the boil in small saucepan. Remove from heat; stir in juice.
nutritional count per serving 21.3g total fat (3.7g saturated fat); 2855kJ (683 cal); 75g carbohydrate; 43.8g protein; 5.3g fibre

We used blue-eye fillets for this recipe but you can use any firm white fish fillet. Tempura batter mix is a blend of wheat and rice flours, starch and spices that allows you to create an authentic Japanese vegetable or seafood tempura easily at home. It is available from Asian grocery stores.

You might need more nori, depending on the size of the fish fillets.

We used frozen soft shell mud crabs; thaw in the fridge overnight. Drain and dry them well before frying to prevent splattering.

on the table in **35 MIN** serves **4**

SOFT SHELL CRAB WITH PAK CHOY AND CHILLI SAUCE

½ cup (75g) cornflour
1 tablespoon ground peri peri
1 tablespoon lemon pepper seasoning
2 tablespoons finely grated lemon rind
2 eggs, beaten lightly
4 soft shell crabs (500g), drained, halved
vegetable oil, for deep-frying
2 tablespoons peanut oil
600g baby pak choy, leaves separated
115g baby corn
CHILLI SAUCE
½ cup (125ml) oyster sauce
2 tablespoons chilli jam
¼ cup (60ml) water

1 Make chilli sauce.
2 Combine cornflour, spices and rind in medium bowl. Dip crab in egg then in spice mixture to coat; shake off excess.
3 Heat vegetable oil in wok; deep-fry crab, in batches, until browned lightly. Remove from wok; drain on absorbent paper.
4 Heat peanut oil in wok; stir-fry pak choy, corn and half the chilli sauce until pak choy wilts, season to taste.
5 Divide pak choy mixture between serving plates; top with crab, drizzle with remaining sauce. Serve with lime wedges.
chilli sauce Combine ingredients in small bowl.
nutritional count per serving 22.4g total fat (3.9g saturated fat); 1852kJ (443 cal); 33.6g carbohydrate; 24.2g protein; 4g fibre

111

SICHUAN DUCK WITH ASPARAGUS

on the table in 25 min serves 4

Combine 600g thinly sliced skinless duck breast with ½ cup sichuan stir-fry sauce in medium bowl. Heat oiled wok; stir-fry duck, in batches, until browned. Remove from wok. Reheat oiled wok; stir-fry 350g coarsely chopped asparagus and 3 cups finely shredded savoy cabbage until cabbage wilts. Return duck to wok with 1 cup frozen peas; stir-fry until peas are hot, season to taste.

nutritional count per serving
16.2g total fat (3.8g saturated fat); 1346kJ (322 cal); 8.9g carbohydrate; 3.2.g protein; 6.3g fibre

Serve with steamed rice.

ANCHOVY, CHILLI AND LIME LAMB

on the table in 25 min serves 4

Combine 600g thinly sliced lamb backstrap, 2 tablespoons chilli jam, 10 finely chopped anchovy fillets, 2 teaspoons finely grated lime rind and ¼ cup lime juice in medium bowl. Heat oiled wok; stir-fry lamb, in batches, until browned. Return lamb to wok; add ¼ cup water to wok; stir-fry until hot, season to taste.

nutritional count per serving
11.9g total fat (3.8g saturated fat); 1091kJ (261 cal); 2.6g carbohydrate; 34.8g protein; 0.9g fibre

Serve lamb with steamed rice or noodles topped with 2 thinly sliced fresh long red chillies.

SALMON IN MISO WITH SOBA NOODLES

on the table in 30 min serves 4

Combine 600g coarsely chopped salmon fillet and 2 tablespoons miso paste in medium bowl. Cook 270g dried soba noodles in medium saucepan of boiling water until tender; drain. Meanwhile, heat oiled wok; stir-fry salmon, in batches, until cooked as desired. Remove from wok. Reheat oiled wok; stir-fry noodles with 2 x 150ml bottles wasabi noodle sauce until hot, season to taste. Serve noodles topped with salmon, 2 thinly sliced green onions and 1 tablespoon salmon roe.

nutritional count per serving
17.4g total fat (3.7g saturated fat); 2312kJ (553 cal); 51.8g carbohydrate; 43.9g protein; 4.5g fibre

CHILLI PRAWNS WITH VERMICELLI NOODLES

on the table in 25 min serves 4

Shell and devein 1kg uncooked medium king prawns, leaving heads and tails intact. Combine prawns with ¼ cup sambal oelek in large bowl. Place 190g rice vermicelli in medium heatproof bowl, cover with boiling water; stand until tender, drain. Heat oiled wok; stir-fry prawns, in batches, until changed in colour. Remove from wok. Reheat oiled wok; stir-fry 420g packet 1-minute stir-fry vegetable mix, 2 thinly sliced long red chillies and 2 tablespoons massaman curry paste until vegetables soften. Return half the prawns to wok with noodles; stir-fry until hot, season to taste. Serve noodles topped with remaining prawns.
nutritional count per serving
9.9g total fat (1.4g saturated fat); 1308kJ (313 cal); 21.3g carbohydrate; 29.7g protein; 9.4g fibre

PEPPERED TUNA WITH ASIAN COLESLAW

on the table in 25 min serves 4

Rub 4 x 150g tuna steaks all over with combined 1 tablespoon each of sweet paprika and coarsely cracked black pepper. Cook tuna on heated oiled grill plate (or grill or barbecue) until cooked as desired. Cover; stand 10 minutes, slice thinly. Meanwhile, heat oiled wok; stir-fry 450g packet coleslaw mix and 2 tablespoons mee goreng paste until vegetables wilt, season to taste. Serve topped with tuna and 100g crispy fried noodles.
nutritional count per serving
18.7g total fat (5.8g saturated fat); 1597kJ (382 cal); 9.7g carbohydrate; 41.7g protein; 4.6g fibre

UDON WITH CHILLI MIXED VEGETABLES

on the table in 20 min serves 4

Place 440g fresh udon noodles in large heatproof bowl, cover with boiling water; separate with fork, drain. Heat oiled wok; stir-fry 400g packet traditional stir-fry vegetables, 100g enoki mushrooms and 2 thinly sliced fresh long red chillies until vegetables wilt. Add noodles and ¼ cup harissa paste; stir-fry until hot, season to taste.
nutritional count per serving
8.1g total fat (1.1g saturated fat); 1083kJ (259 cal); 37.4g carbohydrate; 6.5g protein; 4.7g fibre

GLOSSARY

ALLSPICE also known as pimento or jamaican pepper; so-named because it tastes like a combination of nutmeg, cumin, cinnamon and clove – all spices. Available whole (a small dark brown berry) or ground.

ASIAN GREENS, BABY a mix of baby buk choy, choy sum, gai lan and water spinach. They generally don't store well due to their high water content so it's best to use them on the day of buying.

BACON RASHERS also known as slices of bacon, made from pork side, cured and smoked.

BEAN SPROUTS also known as bean shoots; tender new growths of assorted beans and seeds germinated for consumption as sprouts. The most readily available are mung bean, soya bean, alfalfa and snow pea sprouts.

BEANS, SNAKE long (about 40cm), thin, round, fresh green beans, Asian in origin, with a taste similar to green or french beans; mainly used in stir-fries. Also called yard-long beans because of their (pre-metric) length.

BEEF, RUMP STEAK boneless tender cut taken from the upper part of the hindquarter; similar to sirloin, but slightly less tender.

CAJUN SPICE MIX used to give an authentic American Deep South spicy cajun flavour to food; this packaged blend of assorted herbs and spices can include paprika, basil, onion, fennel, thyme, cayenne and tarragon. Available in supermarkets.

CAPSICUMS also known as bell pepper or, simply, pepper. Native to Central and South America. Comes in many colours: red, green, yellow, orange and purplish-black. Discard seeds and membranes before use.

CHEESE
cheddar a semi-hard cow's-milk cheese. It ranges in colour from white to pale yellow, and has a slightly crumbly texture. Aged for up two years, and the flavour becomes sharper with time.

fetta a crumbly goat's- or sheep's-milk cheese with a sharp salty taste.
haloumi a firm, cream-coloured sheep's-milk cheese matured in brine; somewhat like a minty, salty fetta in flavour. Haloumi must be grilled or fried briefly, and eaten while still warm, as it becomes tough and rubbery on cooling.

CHERMOULA SPICE MIX a North African spice blend that, when sprinkled onto chicken and lamb before cooking, gives a spicy Moroccan-style flavour. A blend of cumin, paprika, onion, turmeric, cayenne pepper, garlic, parsley, salt and pepper.

CHICKPEAS also called garbanzos, channa or hummus; a round, sandy-coloured legume.

CHILLI available in many different types and sizes. Use rubber gloves when seeding and chopping fresh chillies as they can burn your skin. Removing seeds and membranes lessens the heat level.
flakes, dried deep-red, dehydrated chilli slices and whole seeds; good for use in cooking or as a condiment for sprinkling over cooked foods, like salt and pepper.
green usually any unripened chilli, but may include some varieties that are green when ripe, such as jalapeño, habanero, poblano or serrano.
jam a sweet, sourish tangy jam that is sold in jars at supermarkets or Asian food stores. Used in sauces, stir-fries and some soups. After opening, store it in the refrigerator.
long red available both fresh and dried; a generic term used for any moderately hot, long (6cm-8cm), thin chilli.
red thai small, hot and bright red in colour.

CHINESE BARBECUED DUCK traditionally cooked in special ovens, this duck has a sweet-sticky coating made from soy sauce, sherry, five-spice and hoisin sauce. It is available from Asian food stores.

CHINESE BARBECUE PORK also called char siew. Traditionally cooked in special ovens, this pork has a sweet-sticky coating made from soy sauce, sherry, five-spice powder and hoisin sauce. Available from Asian food stores.

CHINESE COOKING WINE also known as hao hsing or chinese rice wine; made from fermented rice, wheat, sugar and salt. A dark straw colour with a unique flavour, it is inexpensive and found in Asian food shops and supermarkets; if you can't find it, use mirin or sherry.

CHORIZO a sausage of Spanish origin; made of coarsely ground pork and highly seasoned with garlic and chillies.

COCONUT
cream is obtained from the first pressing of the coconut flesh alone, without the addition of water.
milk the second pressing (less rich) from grated mature coconut flesh; available in cans and cartons.

CORIANDER both the stems and roots of coriander are used in Thai cooking; wash well before using. Also available ground or as seeds; these should not be substituted for fresh coriander as the tastes are completely different.

CORNFLOUR also known as cornstarch; used as a thickening agent. Available as 100% maize (corn) and wheaten cornflour.

CRANBERRIES, DRIED they have the same slightly sour, succulent flavour as fresh cranberries. Available in most supermarkets.

CUMIN a spice also known as zeera or comino; has a spicy, nutty flavour.

CURRY
curry powder a blend of ground spices; consists of dried chilli, cumin, cinnamon, coriander, fennel, mace, fenugreek, cardamom and turmeric. Can be mild or hot.
massaman curry paste consists of cinnamon, cloves, nutmeg, fish sauce and lemon grass.

red curry paste is milder than the hotter Thai green curry paste. Its ingredients include red chilli, garlic, shallot, salt, lemon grass, galangal, shrimp paste, kaffir lime peel, coriander, cumin and paprika.
singapore hot curry sauce a very hot sauce available from Asian food stores and most major supermarkets.
yellow curry paste one of the mildest Thai pastes; contains mild yellow chilli and fresh turmeric.

EGGPLANT a purple-skinned vegetable also known as aubergine.
baby also known as finger or japanese eggplant; very small and slender.

FIRM WHITE FISH FILLETS any boneless firm white fish fillet – blue eye, bream, swordfish, ling, whiting or sea perch are all good choices. Check for any small pieces of bone in the fillets and use tweezers to remove them.

FIVE-SPICE POWDER (chinese five-spice) a fragrant mixture of ground cinnamon, cloves, sichuan pepper, star anise and fennel seeds.

FLOUR
plain an all-purpose flour made from wheat.
self-raising plain (all-purpose) flour sifted with baking powder in the proportion of 1 cup flour to 2 teaspoons baking powder.

GINGER also known as green or root ginger; the thick root of a tropical plant.
ground also known as powdered ginger; used as a flavouring in cakes and puddings but cannot be substituted for fresh ginger.

HARISSA PASTE a Moroccan paste (or sauce) made from dried chillies, cumin, garlic, oil and caraway seeds. It is available in supermarkets and Middle-Eastern food shops.

LEMON PEPPER also known as lemon pepper seasoning, a blend of crushed black pepper, lemon, herbs and spices.

MINCE also known as ground meat.

MIRIN a Japanese champagne-coloured cooking wine; made of glutinous rice and alcohol and used expressly for cooking. Should not be confused with sake. There is a seasoned sweet mirin called manjo mirin that is made of water, rice, corn syrup and alcohol.

MISO PASTE Japan's famous bean paste made from fermented soya beans and rice, rye or barley. It varies in colour, texture and saltiness. Is a common ingredient in soups, sauces and dressings. *White miso* tends to have a sweeter and somewhat less salty flavour than the darker red miso. *Yellow miso* or yellow bean paste is a thick, deep yellow paste with a fairly salty, but tart, flavour. Dissolve miso in a little water before adding. Keeps well refrigerated. Available from Asian food stores and the Asian food aisle of some of the larger supermarkets.

NASI GORENG SPICE MIX a blend of chilli, ginger, garlic, red chilli, sugar, amchur (dried, powdered green mango), shrimp powder and galangal. It is available from Asian grocery stores and the Asian section of larger supermarkets.

NOODLES
bean thread also known as wun sen and cellophane or glass noodles because they are transparent when cooked. Made from extruded mung bean paste, they are white in colour (not off-white like rice vermicelli), very delicate and fine; available dried in various-sized bundles. Must be soaked to soften before use.
crispy fried are sold packaged (commonly a 100g packet), already deep-fried and ready to eat. May be labelled crunchy noodles.
ramen packaged Japanese instant-style deep-fried wheat noodles, sometimes comes with bits of dehydrated vegetables and broth. Available in various shapes and lengths, and straight or wrinkled. Similar to the instant 2-minute noodles found in supermarkets.

rice vermicelli also known as sen mee, mei fun or bee hoon. Used in spring rolls; similar to bean threads, only longer and made with rice flour instead of mung bean starch. Before using, soak the dried noodles in hot water until softened, then boil them briefly and rinse with hot water.
soba thin Japanese spaghetti-like pale brown noodle made from buckwheat and varying proportions of wheat flour.
singapore these pre-cooked wheat noodles are best described as a thinner version of hokkien; sold, packaged, in the refrigerated section of supermarkets.

NORI a type of dried seaweed used in Japanese cooking as a flavouring, garnish or to make sushi. Sold in thin sheets, plain or toasted (yaki-nori). The thin, dark sheets are usually a dark purplish-black, but they turn green and acquire a pleasant, nutty flavour when toasted. Available from Asian food stores and most supermarkets.

OIL
cooking spray we use a cholesterol-free spray made from canola oil.
olive made from ripened olives. Extra virgin and virgin are the best, while extra light or light refers to taste not fat levels.
peanut pressed from ground peanuts, most commonly used oil in Asian cooking because of its high smoke point (capacity to handle high heat without burning).
sesame made from roasted, crushed, white sesame seeds; used as a flavouring rather than a cooking oil.
vegetable sourced from plants rather than animal fats.

ONIONS
purple shallots also known as asian shallots, pink shallots or homm; thin-layered and intensely flavoured, they are used in cooking throughout South-East Asia.
red also known as red spanish, spanish or bermuda onion; a sweet-flavoured, large, purple-red onion.

PAPRIKA ground dried sweet red capsicum (bell pepper); there are many types available, including sweet, hot, mild and smoked.

PERI PERI see sauces.

PRAWNS also known as shrimp.

SAMBAL OELEK (also ulek or olek) a salty paste made from ground chillies and vinegar.

SAUCES

cantonese classic Cantonese sauces are light, mellow and more bland when compared to the thicker, darker and richer sauces of other Chinese cuisines. Spring onion, sugar, salt, soy sauce, rice wine, cornflour, vinegar, sesame and other oils are used to enhance the flavour. Prepared cantonese sauces are available from Asian grocery stores and supermarkets.

pad thai a Thai-style sauce containing oyster sauce, palm sugar, soy sauce, fish sauce, tamarind and shallots. It has a sweet, salty, spicy flavour.

peri peri (piri piri) a hot spicy Afro-Portuguese chilli sauce, paste or powder, is available from major supermarkets and spice stores.

soy also known as sieu, is made from fermented soya beans. Several variations are available in most supermarkets and Asian food stores. We use Japanese soy in our recipes unless indicated otherwise; it is possibly the best table soy and the one to choose if you only want one variety.

tamari a thick, dark soy sauce made mainly from soya beans without the wheat used in standard soy sauces.

sweet and sour a blend of onions, tomatoes, capsicum, pineapple, carrots and selected spices. Available from supermarkets.

tomato also known as ketchup.

tomato pasta a prepared sauce made from a blend of tomatoes, herbs and spices.

worcestershire a dark coloured sauce made from garlic, soy sauce, tamarind, onions, molasses, lime, anchovies, vinegar and seasonings.

SESAME SEEDS, BLACK these sesame seeds are the un-hulled seeds; they may be either black or golden brown. Black sesame seeds are available from speciality spice shops and some delicatessens.

SHIITAKE MUSHROOMS when dried are known as donko or dried chinese mushrooms; rehydrate before use.

SHRIMP PASTE also known as trasi and blanchan; a strong-scented, almost solid preserved paste made of salted dried shrimp. Used as a pungent flavouring in many South-East Asian soups and sauces. Use it sparingly because a little goes a long way. It can be wrapped in foil and heated before using to release its pungent aroma and flavour.

SNOW PEAS also called mange tout ("eat all").

snow pea sprouts tender new growths of snow peas; these are also known as mange tout.

SUGAR

brown a very soft, finely granulated sugar retaining molasses for its characteristic colour and flavour.

caster also known as superfine or finely granulated table sugar.

palm also known as nam tan pip, jaggery, jawa or gula melaka; made from the sap of the sugar palm tree. Light brown to black in colour and usually sold in rock-hard cakes; the sugar of choice in Indian and most South-East Asian cooking. Substitute it with brown sugar if unavailable.

SUGAR SNAP PEAS also known as honey snap peas; fresh small pea that can be eaten whole, pod and all, similarly to snow peas.

TAMARI see sauces.

TAMARIND the tamarind tree produces clusters of hairy brown pods, each filled with seeds and a viscous pulp that are dried and pressed into the blocks of tamarind found in Asian food shops. Gives a sweet-sour, slightly astringent taste to sauces and dressings.

TAMARIND CONCENTRATE the distillation of tamarind pulp into a condensed paste; adds a tart sour taste to dishes. Found in Asian food stores and supermarkets.

TEMPURA BATTER MIX an authentic Japanese blend of wheat and rice flours, starch and spices that allows you to create tempura seafood or vegetables quickly and easily.

TOFU also known as bean curd, an off-white, custard-like product made from the "milk" of crushed soya beans; comes fresh as soft or firm. Leftover fresh tofu can be refrigerated in water (which is changed daily) for up to four days.

firm made by compressing bean curd to remove most of the water. Good used in stir-fries because it can be tossed without falling apart.

silken refers to the method by which it is made – where it is strained through silk.

VINEGAR

brown malt made from fermented malt and beech shavings.

chinese black a deep, dark vinegar that has a complex, smoky, malty flavour that works well in stir-fries, braises and marinades. It is available from Asian grocery stores and some larger supermarkets.

rice a colourless vinegar made from fermented rice and flavoured with sugar and salt. Also known as seasoned rice vinegar.

white made from the spirit of cane sugar.

WASABI a Japanese horseradish available as a paste in tubes or powdered in tins from Asian food stores and many supermarkets.

WILD RICE BLEND a packaged mixture of white long-grain and dark brown wild rice. The latter is the seed of a North American aquatic grass; it has a distinctively nutty flavour and a crunchy, resilient texture.

ZUCCHINI also known as courgette; small, pale- or dark-green, yellow or white vegetable belonging to the squash family.

CONVERSION CHART

MEASURES

One Australian metric measuring cup holds approximately 250ml; one Australian metric tablespoon holds 20ml; one Australian metric teaspoon holds 5ml.

The difference between one country's measuring cups and another's is within a two- or three-teaspoon variance, and will not affect your cooking results. North America, New Zealand and the United Kingdom use a 15ml tablespoon.

All cup and spoon measurements are level. The most accurate way of measuring dry ingredients is to weigh them. When measuring liquids, use a clear glass or plastic jug with the metric markings.

We use large eggs with an average weight of 60g.

DRY MEASURES

METRIC	IMPERIAL
15g	½oz
30g	1oz
60g	2oz
90g	3oz
125g	4oz (¼lb)
155g	5oz
185g	6oz
220g	7oz
250g	8oz (½lb)
280g	9oz
315g	10oz
345g	11oz
375g	12oz (¾lb)
410g	13oz
440g	14oz
470g	15oz
500g	16oz (1lb)
750g	24oz (1½lb)
1kg	32oz (2lb)

LIQUID MEASURES

METRIC	IMPERIAL
30ml	1 fluid oz
60ml	2 fluid oz
100ml	3 fluid oz
125ml	4 fluid oz
150ml	5 fluid oz (¼ pint/1 gill)
190ml	6 fluid oz
250ml	8 fluid oz
300ml	10 fluid oz (½ pint)
500ml	16 fluid oz
600ml	20 fluid oz (1 pint)
1000ml (1 litre)	1¾ pints

LENGTH MEASURES

METRIC	IMPERIAL
3mm	⅛in
6mm	¼in
1cm	½in
2cm	¾in
2.5cm	1in
5cm	2in
6cm	2½in
8cm	3in
10cm	4in
13cm	5in
15cm	6in
18cm	7in
20cm	8in
23cm	9in
25cm	10in
28cm	11in
30cm	12in (1ft)

OVEN TEMPERATURES

These oven temperatures are only a guide for conventional ovens. For fan-forced ovens, check the manufacturer's manual.

	°C (CELSIUS)	°F (FAHRENHEIT)	GAS MARK
Very slow	120	250	½
Slow	150	275-300	1-2
Moderately slow	160	325	3
Moderate	180	350-375	4-5
Moderately hot	200	400	6
Hot	220	425-450	7-8
Very hot	240	475	9

INDEX

Published in 2010 by ACP Books, Sydney
ACP Books are published by ACP Magazines
a division of PBL Media Pty Limited

ACP BOOKS

General manager Christine Whiston
Editor-in-chief Susan Tomnay
Creative director & designer Hieu Chi Nguyen
Art director Hannah Blackmore
Senior editor Wendy Bryant
Food director Pamela Clark
Sales & rights director Brian Cearnes
Marketing manager Bridget Cody
Senior business analyst Rebecca Varela
Circulation manager Jama Mclean
Operations manager David Scotto
Production manager Victoria Jefferys

Published by ACP Books, a division of ACP Magazines Ltd,
54 Park St, Sydney; GPO Box 4088, Sydney, NSW 2001.
phone (02) 9282 8618; fax (02) 9267 9438.

acpbooks@acpmagazines.com.au;
www.acpbooks.com.au

Printed by Toppan Printing Co, China.

Australia Distributed by Network Services,
phone +61 2 9282 8777; fax +61 2 9264 3278;
networkweb@networkservicescompany.com.au
United Kingdom Distributed by Australian Consolidated Press (UK),
phone (01604) 642 200; fax (01604) 642 300; books@acpuk.com
New Zealand Distributed by Netlink Distribution Company,
phone (9) 366 9966; ask@ndc.co.nz
South Africa Distributed by PSD Promotions,
phone (27 11) 392 6065/6/7; fax (27 11) 392 6079/80; orders@psdprom.co.za
Canada Distributed by Publishers Group Canada
phone (800) 663 5714; fax (800) 565 3770; service@raincoast.com

Wok simple / food director Pamela Clark.
ISBN: 978 1 74245 007 0 (pbk.)
Notes: Includes index.
Subjects: Wok cookery.
Other Authors/Contributors: Clark, Pamela.
Also Titled: Australian women's weekly.
Dewey Number: 641.77
© ACP Magazines Ltd 2010
ABN 18 053 273 546
This publication is copyright. No part of it may be reproduced or transmitted
in any form without the written permission of the publishers.

Recipe development Dominic Smith, Lucy Nunes, Nicole Jennings
Nutritional information Nicole Jennings
Photographer Dean Wilmot
Stylist Trish Hegarty
Food preparation Dom Smith; Amal Webster
Cover Almond and chilli chicken, page 72

The publishers would like to thank the following for props used in photography
Bison Homewares, Ikea, KifKaf, Malcolm Greenwo...

Scanpan cookware is used in the ...

To order books
phone 136 116 (within A...
order online at www.acpbo...
Send recipe enquiries ...
recipeenquiries@acpmagazi...